PHANTOM GOURMET®

Guide to Boston's Best Restaurants

2013

PhantomGourmet.com

ISBN-13: 978-0-9882924-0-6

First Edition: November 2012

10 9 8 7 6 5 4 3 2 1

Contents

Great Ates by Category

Contents

Great Ates by Location

Great Ate Guide to using this book:

1) This book contains 500 of New England's best restaurants.

2) The restaurants are categorized by your favorite cuisine types and destinations (eight favorites for each).

3) The list of categories (first cuisine types, then destinations) is at the front of the book.

4) There's an alphabetical list of restaurants at the back of the book. There is also a list by location.

5) Each restaurant listing has the address, phone number, and website. We recommend calling first, as restaurants sometimes close, change their hours, change their menu, etc.

6) Each restaurant can only be in ONE category (for instance, a restaurant can't be in both Seafood and Lobster).

7) We try to provide a variety of price ranges and/or locations for each category.

8) Please remember, only restaurants listed on *PhantomGourmet.com/GiftCard* accept the Phantom Gourmet Restaurant Gift Card. NOT every restaurant in this book, PhantomGourmet.com, or on television or radio accepts the card.

PHANTOM GOURMET®

GREAT ATES

by Category

Asian
GREAT ATE

Sapporo

50 East Main St., Westboro, MA (508) 898-1880

www.sapporobbq.com

Sapporo is a spacious suburban restaurant offering a mix of Japanese sushi, Chinese appetizers and authentic Korean BBQ, including grills built right into the tables. For a true interactive Asian experience, diners can order meats and vegetables and cook them to their liking as they drink and dine. The sushi ranges from typical to over the top, including the Avocado Ball: a succulent sphere of tuna tartare that's wrapped in creamy avocado and crunchy tempura with a side of tortilla chips for dipping.

Pho Lemongrass

239 Harvard St., Brookline, MA (617) 731-8600

www.pholemongrass.com

Pho Lemongrass is a low-key eatery with a sprawling mural of Vietnamese waterscapes across the back wall. This is a fine place to restore your spirits with the national dish of Vietnam, pho. Pho is a steaming soup of beef broth and noodles loaded with steak, basil, cilantro and sprouts. Not only is there soup, Pho Lemongrass also has plenty of other Vietnamese cuisine like noodles, rice, curry, stir-fry and more. For dessert, Phantom loves the Chui Chien Fried Bananas, a sugary explosion of fruit topped with honey rum sauce.

Bon Chon

123 Brighton Ave., Allston, MA (617) 254-8888

57 JFK St., Cambridge, MA (617) 868-0981

www.bonchon.com

Bon Chon has become a worldwide food phenomenon. The concept was created in South Korea and quickly spread to Singapore, Dubai, Hong Kong, Thailand and finally to Massachusetts. The must have menu item is the Bon Chon Chicken that's double-fried so it's crispy and never greasy. It's prepared three ways: fresh white meat strips, extra-crunchy wings or jumbo drumsticks. Customers can choose from sweet soy garlic or addictively fiery hot sauce that's hand painted one strip at a time. Beyond chicken, Bon Chon offers a variety of

Asian fare like Korean bulgogi or bibimbap and super fresh sushi.

Foumami

225 Franklin St., Boston, MA (617) 426-8858

www.foumami.com

Foumami is an inventive Asian sandwich bar offering the hungry diners of downtown Boston sandwiches served on shaobing, a Chinese bread with a fluffy center and crunchy exterior. With quick counter service, this futuristic takeout spot provides slow cooked sandwiches served fast. The grilled rib eye sandwich is marinated in a tangy Korean BBQ sauce and topped with scallions, cucumber and cilantro. The spicy pork loin sandwich is a twist on Vietnamese bahn mi. For a taste of Tokyo, try the crispy chicken katsu.

Wagamama

800 Boylston St., Boston, MA (617) 778-2344

1 Faneuil Hall, Boston, MA (617) 742-9242

57 JFK St., Cambridge, MA (617) 499-0930

www.wagamama.us

A London-based noodle bar, Wagamama serves big bowls of noodle soup in a fun, sleek setting that students can afford and businessman love on their lunch break. Framed in a gorgeous glass space, the atmosphere is sleek and modern, yet still quite casual with communal wood tables throughout the dining room. Loads of Asian inspired noodles fill the menu in soups, spicy sauces, teppan griddle-fried plates and salads. Familiar desserts with a flavorful Asian twist include sweet coconut ice cream drizzled with tangy mango sauce and light-as-air citrus lime mousse on a buttery shortbread cookie.

Bamboo

213 Burlington Rd., Bedford, MA (781) 275-5888

55 Ariadne Rd., Dedham, MA (781) 251-2566

1 Lan Drive, Westford, MA (978) 589-9666

www.bamboogourmet.com

Bamboo is a stylish and spacious Pan-Asian restaurant with a kitchen that cranks out tons of takeout orders and wok after wok of fresh-cooked, high-quality dishes. There are lettuce wraps with your choice of chicken or shrimp, fresh Vietnamese summer rolls and yellowtail tuna in a sweet chili sauce. The "Bo Bo for Two" is an impressive sampler, stacked with shrimp tempura, crab rangoon, beef skewers and a mound of sticky-sweet boneless spare ribs. As for the entrees, the sizzling platter of beef and scallops is served smoking hot with mushrooms and mixed vegetables and the Tropical Taste Chicken is a refreshing blend of pineapple and peppers. On the Japanese side of the menu, Bamboo offers everything from an ultra-tender steak teriyaki to colorful Lobster Maki stuffed with spicy tuna and avocado.

House of Siam

542 Columbus Ave., Boston, MA (617) 267-1755

592 Tremont St., Boston, MA (617) 267-7426

www.houseofsiamboston.com

House of Siam has been a South End staple for years. Both locations cook everything to order so you can have it as spicy or as mild as you want. The most popular dish is the Pad Thai. It's authentically prepared with rice noodles, chicken, shrimp and ground peanuts. For a little twist, the Crispy Pad Thai substitutes sticky-sweet, deep-fried rice noodles that are extra crunchy. The tasty, toasty Golden Bags are like a little present for your mouth, stuffed with ground chicken, onions and sweet corn. The atmosphere is casual, but the space is intimate enough to have a romantic date. If you want takeout or delivery, owner "Joe Thailand" will make it happen fast and fresh.

Penang

685 Washington St., Boston, MA (617) 451-6373

Unlike most Chinatown restaurants, Penang is an absolutely beautiful, sparkling clean spot featuring a ceiling decked out with lots of bamboo, ropes and exposed brick. Malaysian cuisine is the focus, serving a flavorful combination of Chinese and Indian flavors. Some of the standout dishes include the Beef Satay, Roti Cania with chicken curry dip, and tropical Mango Chicken. There's also a wide selection of fresh fish and incredibly fragrant pineapple fried rice. For such a busy and refined restaurant, service is incredibly quick and the prices (although a bit steep for the neighborhood) are quite reasonable considering the quality.

Bakeries
GREAT ATE

Lyndell's

720 Broadway, Somerville, MA (617) 625-1793

74 Prospect St., Cambridge, MA (617) 576-3530

www.lyndells.com

Dating back to 1887, Lyndell's Bakery is still worth its weight in cake flour. You may be tempted by the Italian pastries, but don't dare leave without a half moon in hand. This black and white cookie is for icing lovers only, with a fluffy cake supporting twice as much vanilla and chocolate frosting as the standard version you'd find somewhere else. Lyndell's cookie selection includes molasses, praline and butter crunch varieties. They also do honey dipped donuts, incredible cinnamon buns, frosted cupcakes and flaky elephant ears. Rainbow birthday cakes line the front windows and the staff uses an old school string dispenser to wrap the boxes.

PB Boulangerie Bistro

15 Lecount Hollow Rd., South Wellfleet, MA (508) 349-1600

www.pbboulangeriebistro.com

PB Boulangerie is an authentic French bakery serving the kind of buttery croissants, rustic breads and indulgent treats that carb-lovers long for. The trays of pastries, stacks of cookies and shelves lined with bread are all made in the old fashioned, old world style. Getting there early is important, as it's not uncommon for customers to wait over an hour in a line stretching out the door. For a dinner experience, PB Boulangerie also has a real deal French bistro attached, where the sounds of an antique, hand cranked music box fill your ears and the smells of authentic French fare arouse your appetite.

Frederick's Pastries

119 Main St., North Andover, MA (978) 208-7806

109 State Rte. 101A, Amherst, NH (603) 882-7725

25 South River Rd., Bedford, NH (603) 647-2253

www.pastry.net

Frederick's is a mini bakery chain that, much like Phantom, has a passion for all things purple. There's vibrant purple velvet cake, purple cake truffles, purple cheesecake and even purple wedding cakes. Other creative confections include chocolate M&M cups, chocolate covered potato chips and colossal cupcakes filled with maple buttercream. Even the whoopie pies are made with a twist. Rather than cake, Frederick's takes whatever cookies were baked that day and sandwiches them around buttercream frosting.

D. Palmieri's Bakery

624 Killingly St., Johnston, RI (401) 621-9357

www.dpalmierisbakery.com

This classic family run Italian bakery has been leaving locals' mouths watering for decades. They do it all from sweet pastries to Rhode Island pizza strips: a thick-crusted Sicilian style dough topped with sauce and oregano that's served at room temperature. The sauce is so good, cheese is just not necessary on this pizza. In fact, the sauce is so popular, it's jarred and sold to customers who try to pass it off as their own. D. Palmieri's cooks all their meatballs in that same sauce before they're stuffed into fresh sub rolls or served straight up. While takeout is popular, there are a few seats both inside and out to enjoy it all.

Modern Pastry

257 Hanover St., Boston, MA (617) 523-3783

20 Salem St., Medford, MA (781) 396-3618

www.modernpastry.com

One of the North End's oldest pastry shops, Modern Pastry makes the best cannoli this side of Sicily. Crispy tubes of deep fried pastry shell are filled to order and hand dipped in chocolate or almonds. Other Italian specialties include colorful cookies and almond marzipan shaped into peaches, watermelon and cherries. Modern makes masterful ricotta pie and specialty cakes. There are only a few seats, so plan on taking your sweets to go. There's a second location in Medford that has more street parking than the Boston store.

Petsi Pies

285 Beacon St., Somerville, MA (617) 661-7437

31 Putnam Ave., Cambridge, MA (617) 499-0801

www.petsipies.com

Petsi Pies is a small storefront turning out perfect pies. Their secret lies in the rich, flaky crust baked to a golden hue. The apple pie is nothing short of awesome, but there are also sticky, sweet pecan pie and walnut fudge brownies. The house specialties are all Southern, including sweet potato pie spiced with ginger and brown sugar. Phantom loves the peach blueberry pie bursting with ripe fruit and the potato mushroom tart layered with roasted red bliss potatoes, fresh rosemary and Gruyere cheese.

Danish Pastry House

330 Boston Ave., Medford, MA (781) 396-8999

205 Arlington St., Watertown, MA (617) 926-2747

www.danishpastryhouse.com

Danish Pastry House serves all the sweets you'd find if you took a trip to Denmark. This super authentic shop carries everything Danes crave like crepes stuffed with strawberries, bananas and Nutella, fresh fruit cups topped with lemon whipped cream and sinful homemade Pop Tarts. Every day of the week, the Danish Pastry House makes great pastries for breakfast and awesome sandwiches for lunch. The must try item is the Kringle, a traditional dessert that has a flaky pastry exterior and almond paste inside. The Medford location is set up like a European Cafe and has plenty of seating while the Watertown location is takeout only.

Tripoli Bakery

106 Common St., Lawrence, MA (978) 682-7754

542 Turnpike St., North Andover, MA (978) 682-0003

19 Broadway, Salisbury, MA (978) 465-3846

418 Rte.286, Seabrook, NH (603) 474-7764

www.tripolibakery.com

Tripoli is the ultimate old time Italian bakery. For over eighty years, the Zappala family has been kneading, baking and frosting their way into the hearts and stomachs of everyone they meet. The display cases are always full of mouthwatering treats like decadent cakes stuffed with a thick layer of creamy filling. Tripoli is famous for Lobster Tail pastries, exploding with a blend of homemade whipped cream and ricotta cheese. There's also a crispier version of fried dough known as "Guandi." While Phantom can't get enough of Tripoli's sweets, it's the Super Stick that really impresses. This giant baguette is perfect for parties and gatherings.

Bargains
GREAT ATE

Belle Isle Seafood

1 Main St., Winthrop, MA (617) 539-1619

www.belleisleseafood.com

Located at the edge of East Boston, just over the Winthrop line, Belle Isle is a laid back seafood spot serving fresh, amazing fish at bargain basement prices. Customers come for the fresh haddock, which is picked up at the pier every morning. There's homemade chowder loaded with clams. The fish and chips is always made with fresh haddock. Swordfish can be prepared five different ways, including Cajun Blackened. The Fisherman's Platter is piled high with haddock, scallops, shrimp and clams and the ultra- affordable lobster roll is absolutely loaded with succulent meat.

Byblos

678 Washington St., Norwood, MA (781) 278-0000

www.byblosrestaurant.com

Byblos may be the most delicious, authentic and affordable Middle Eastern restaurant in New England. Lebanese music plays in the background while customers feast on fragrant dishes in the expansive dining room. Named after an ancient Lebanese port city, Byblos keeps the cuisine traditional and flavorful. Hummus and baba ghanoush fly out of the kitchen along with sizzling hot grilled kebobs. The tabbouleh is a lemony bulgur wheat salad with ripe tomatoes and parsley and the fattoush salad combines cucumbers, scallions, radishes and toasted pitas. The portions are huge and meant to be shared, so you can fill up on flavorful fare without spending too much.

Alex's Chimis

358 Centre St., Jamaica Plain, MA (617) 522-5201

www.alexschimisrestaurant.com

Alex's Chimis is a small space that's big on takeout. There's counter service and a few tables for dining on their famous, golden brown rotisserie chicken. Each bird is slow cooked and seasoned to perfection. The "chimis" are essentially a Dominican version of a hamburger. Each one is topped with green tomatoes (rather than red), cabbage (rather than lettuce) and plenty of mayo and ketchup.

Freshly squeezed juices like passion fruit, tamarind and lemonade are a good choice to pair with your meal. With no chimis more than five bucks and a half chicken with two sides at eight dollars, Alex's is tasty and cheap.

Emma's Pub & Pizza

1420 Pleasant St., Bridgewater, MA (508) 697-8815

130 Mansfield Ave., Norton, MA (508) 285-8814

128 Broad St., Bridgewater, MA (508) 697-6674

www.emmaspubandpizza.com

People who frequent Emma's Pub & Pizza can only assume owner, "Crazy" Ron Emma, has lost his mind because the prices are just unbelievably low. For twenty-six years, this casual restaurant has been a great place for big draft beers, tons of TVs, free popcorn at the bar, and wallet friendly meals in the dining room. There are all your comfort food favorites like pizza, sandwiches, burgers and specials that change throughout the week. While all the portions are big, you're going to need to bring your appetite for the Titanic Lobster Roll bursting with a half pound of meat and the twenty ounce portion of juicy steak tips. For takeout, the twenty-four inch sheet pan pizza is perfect for parties.

Eight/10 Bar and Grill

8 Norwood St., Everett, MA (617) 387-9810

www.eight10barandgrille.com

The Eight/10 is a casual restaurant with hardwood floors, red and white tablecloths and a constantly crowded bar. The menu consists of straightforward American favorites like roast turkey dinners, meatloaf, mac and cheese and American chop suey. Italian entrees like chicken parm, penne a la vodka and ravioli come in ridiculously sized portions. The pizzas aren't only delicious, they're inexpensive with the Shrimp Scampi Pizza topping off at fifteen bucks. The dessert menu features Italian favorites like tiramisu or the limoncello flute. Phantom always orders the Coppa Mascarpone which has chocolate and mascarpone cream topped with sweet cookie crumbs.

Frank's Steak House

2310 Massachusetts Ave., Cambridge, MA (617) 661-0666

www.frankssteakhouse.com

Opened in 1938, Frank's is the oldest steak house in Greater Boston. While the prices are about half what you'd pay at the other city steak houses, the quality is second to none. Phantom loves "The Sizzler": a sixteen ounce hand cut boneless

NY Strip served on a smoking hot cast iron skillet. The steaks come with sides and top off at twenty-three bucks. Appetizers like golden fried chicken fingers, crunchy Bruschetta and gooey French onion soup ring in at around six bucks, and a warm brownie sundae with vanilla ice cream and hot fudge is about four. There's a small parking lot in the back if you can't find a metered spot on the street.

Real Deal

736 Centre St., Jamaica Plain, MA (617) 522-1181

1882 Centre St., West Roxbury, MA (617) 325-0754

www.realdealdeli.net

Real Deal is a quirky, counter service sandwich shop with cartoon murals dedicated to the food. This casual space serves well over a hundred sandwiches, almost all of which cost under eight bucks. There are popular favorites like the roast beef, steak and cheese and Reubens. An entire section of the menu lists "Gangster Wraps", like the Henry Hill with smoked turkey, Swiss, bacon, and chipotle mayo. The Al "Scarface" Capone contains a chicken cutlet, feta and Greek dressing. Beyond sandwiches, other options include spicy Buffalo wings, pizza, salads and big burgers like The Frankenstein. This one pound gut bomb of a burger is served in a sub roll topped with American cheese. All the breads are baked fresh daily at their sister store, Sugar Bakery.

The Chicken Connection

242 Broadway, Haverhill, MA (978) 373-4300

www.thechickenconnection.com

For almost twenty years, the Chicken Connection has been an institution in the town of Haverhill. It looks like a house from the outside, but inside you'll find warm, yellow walls with a few booths and counter seats. The restaurant is super casual, serving most everything on paper plates. The fried chicken is always fresh, never frozen. The breading is very light but incredibly crispy and each piece is perfectly fried, plump and juicy. There's also rotisserie chicken, chicken soup, chicken pies, chicken wings and chicken fingers. All dinners come with a choice of two homestyle sides like mashed potatoes, butternut squash, mac and cheese, cornbread stuffing and crispy red bliss potatoes with lemon pepper seasoning.

Blue Ribbon Bar-B-Q

908 Massachusetts Ave., Arlington, MA (781) 648-7427

1375 Washington St., West Newton, MA (617) 332-2583

www.blueribbonbbq.com

With a restaurant in Arlington and a smaller, mostly takeout shop in West Newton, Blue Ribbon Bar-B-Q serves some of the best BBQ in all New England. The down home Southern inspired space is clad with old license plates and sassy signs. The majority of the menu is blue ribbon worthy, but the pulled pork sandwich rises above the rest. The pork is cooked slow and low and then shredded, North Carolina style. The sandwich is such a delicious hot mess, you're better off eating it with a fork and knife. Add in some tangy baked beans and creamy coleslaw, and you'll be in barbecue bliss. Beer and BBQ lovers please note: The Arlington location does not serve alcohol.

Firefly's Bar-B-Que

350 East Main St., Marlboro, MA (508) 357-8883

235 Old Connecticut Path, Framingham, MA (508) 820-3333

www.fireflysbbq.com

Firefly's is a big, bustling restaurant where low and slow cooking is an art. Hickory, cherry and apple woods smoke the meats, which are already packed with intensity from dry spice rubs. For added flavor, the condiment bar includes five sauces (North or South Carolina, Memphis, spicy Beelzebar and Texas), assorted pickles and forty hot sauces. The grilled Cracklin' Bread is awesome, topped with onions and smoked mozzarella. The incredibly tasty St. Louis style ribs are served with two sides and cornbread. Other addictive Firefly's favorites include the jumbo wings basted with honey cayenne hot sauce, crispy buttermilk Southern fried chicken, sweet bourbon marinated turkey tips and pizzas topped with everything from apple smoked bacon to Andouille sausage.

Bison County

275 Moody St., Waltham, MA (781) 642-9720

www.bisoncounty.com

At Bison County, Texas and Southern-style BBQ are cooked on an eight foot open grill in the middle of the dining room. A meal feels like a visit to the old West, especially if you saddle up to their big ol' bar stocked with sixty beers, dozens of single malt scotches and single barrel bourbons. Nothing goes better with a good drink than some great snacks like Smoked Pork Egg Rolls with Jack cheese, hand breaded fried pickles with barbecue and horseradish dipping sauces or golden fritters studded with sweet corn. A snack you'll most definitely want to attack is the South Carolina wings dripping with a mustard-based barbecue sauce. Since this is Bison Country, you may also want to consider an order of Bozeman Bison Tips, which are flavorful yet low in fat and cholesterol.

The American Barbeque

5 Railroad Ave., Rowley, MA (978) 948-2626

950 Cummings Center, Beverly, MA (978) 921-1212

www.tabbq.com

The American Barbeque is festively decorated with nostalgic Americana, exposed wood beams and little pigs everywhere you look. Customers come for the sliced brisket platter piled high with creamy mac and cheese. The St. Louis ribs are truly tender and the plate-tipping pulled chicken sandwich is served with sweet potato fries. In true southern style, meals don't come slathered with sauce because the meat is so tender and juicy, you only need a little on the side.

Soul Fire Barbecue

182 Harvard Ave., Allston, MA (617) 787-3003

737 Huntington Ave., Boston, MA (617) 232-8000

www.soulfirebbq.com

"Serving all souls," Soul Fire Barbecue appeals to heat seekers with an appetite for brisket, pulled pork and baby back ribs. The regional BBQ is pit smoked with a dry rub. Customers decide on the final slather from homemade sauces at the self-service BBQ bar. Choose from their signature Soul Fire Sauce, vinegar-based North Carolina hot sauce, South Carolina mustard sauce and chili pepper Fiery Sauce. On the side, Southern Fried Mac and Cheese Bites are Phantom's dream appetizer come true. The crispy, crunchy nuggets are gooey inside and absolutely irresistible dipped in molasses sweet sauce.

East Coast Grill & Raw Bar

1271 Cambridge St., Cambridge, MA (617) 491-6568

www.eastcoastgrill.net

East Coast Grill in Inman Square is a fun, funky eatery with island and underwater colors, a lively marble bar at the entrance and plastic fish pinned to the walls. High energy emanates from the open kitchen, while blackboard menus mesh with the casual atmosphere. They offer all the usual BBQ favorites like pulled pork, brisket and ribs. The kitchen also specializes in grilled seafood, like their White Pepper Crusted Tuna or the Spice Crusted Mahi Mahi. If you truly want to tantalize your taste buds, stop in on a Sunday when they set up a Bloody Mary buffet with additions like celery stalks, salsas, pickled vegetables and more to customize the quintessential brunch beverage.

Redbones

55 Chester St., Somerville, MA (617) 628-2200

www.redbonesbbq.com

Covering the full sweep of the barbecue belt, Redbones has the best regional renditions of Texas beef, St. Louis ribs and Georgia pulled pork. Redbones is the most famous BBQ restaurant in Greater Boston, and once you've tried it, you'll know why. Tantalizing appetizers include the sausage of the day, hush puppies, Buffalo shrimp and corn fritters. An eclectic crowd of bikers, families and singles pack the psychedelic neon den downstairs, while drinkers buzz about the bar upstairs where the microbrews on tap change daily. The key lime pie is a tangy treat to round out your meal.

Little Red Smokehouse

145 South Main St., Carver, MA (508) 465-0018

www.littleredsmokehouse.com

With a name like the Little Red Smokehouse, it's no surprise that this rustic and casual restaurant serves some tremendous Southern style barbecue. The pork butts are smoked so perfectly, they can be shredded by hand. The brisket drips with deliciousness and ribs are pull from the bone tender. Sides are just as special, from the stuffed sweet potato topped with mini marshmallows to the jumbo homemade tater tots. The dessert menu includes one of the most over the top endings Phantom has ever seen. The Deep Fried Caramel Apple Sundae is a Granny Smith apple that's spiral cut, beer battered, deep fried and plated with vanilla bean ice cream, fresh whipped cream and warm caramel sauce.

Beer Lovers
GREAT ATE

Boston Beer Works

61 Brookline Ave., Boston, MA (617) 536-2337

112 Canal St., Boston, MA (617) 896-2337

www.beerworks.net

As Boston's oldest and biggest restaurant-brewery, Boston Beer Works sports an industrial interior where all the brewing equipment is in full view. Sports fans feel right at home, with flat screen TVs covering every angle, amazing snacks to munch on and an entire wall devoted to beer bottles. The menu is absolutely enormous, with plenty of pizzas, burgers, steak tips, fish and chips and meatloaf. But, it's the Bunker Hill Blueberry Beer that's the true spectacle, with fresh Maine blueberries dancing around in that sweet amber elixir. The Brookline Ave location is right at the entrance of Fenway Park and perfect for a pregame beer. There are additional spots in Salem, Lowell and Hingham.

Sunset Grill & Tap

130 Brighton Ave., Allston, MA (617) 254-1331

www.allstonsfinest.com

The Sunset Grill & Tap is serious about beer with 112 taps and 380 microbrews. This loud, festive location offers it all, from seasonals and ciders to cask ales. Order a flight to sample a few or go "all in" and order a whole yard. The kitchen stays open until 1am, so you won't have to worry about finding some food to go with your beverage. There are steamed beer burgers alongside crispy curly fries, slow-cooked baby back ribs and spicy Buffalo wings. During dinner hours, expect a wait because this lively spot is usually filled to the gills with college kids chowing down on fairly priced fare.

Yard House

200 Legacy Place, Dedham, MA (781) 326-4644

126 Brookline Ave., Boston, MA (617) 236-4083

www.yardhouse.com

Like the male equivalent of the Cheesecake Factory, this brew house serves 120 menu items and 130 draft beers. From microbrews to the names you know, be prepared to be overwhelmed. The restaurant gets its name from the towering thirty-two ounce yard glasses they use to serve the beer. The food menu is just as large. There are forty appetizers including three kinds of wings, a beer battered onion ring tower and overloaded chicken nachos. There's also hand tossed pizza, outrageous burgers and more upscale dishes like the pepper crusted filet mignon. With classic rock blaring from above and your favorite sports displayed in HD, the Yard House is the ultimate adult playground.

Horseshoe Pub

29 South St., Hudson, MA (978) 568-1265

www.horseshoepub.com

Located on the back roads of a small town in Central Massachusetts, the Horseshoe Pub is a comfortable, friendly tavern serving comfort food to a fun, lively crowd. With over eighty taps and two cask ales, the Horseshoe boasts one of the biggest beer selections in New England. Each pairs beautifully with pub fare like towering Irish nachos featuring waffle fries, melted cheese and chopped bacon. The creative Reuben eggrolls are unexpected, stuffed with corned beef and cabbage and served with Russian dressing. However, nothing makes Phantom's belly growl like the five cheese mac and cheese, served warm and bubbly in a skillet. The fried dough sundae is an over the top way to round out your meal, with a crunchy fried dough bowl holding plenty of ice cream and hot fudge.

The British Beer Company

www.britishbeer.com

With ten Massachusetts locations from Framingham to Falmouth, the British Beer Company brings a taste of England to New England. They offer almost forty beers on tap and well over a hundred by the bottle. Of course, proper ID is required if you want to drink, but you'll also need your license to order the "Over 21 Pizza". This intoxicating pie is topped with steak, peppers, onions, and mushrooms and finished tableside with a liberal spritz of bourbon. The kitchen cranks out British favorites like Bangers and Mash, and classic fish and chips with a perfect beer batter. There's also stateside fare like burgers, wraps, ribs and tips. Whether you grab a stool at the handmade mahogany bar imported from London or slide into one of the high top booths, this is a place where customers love to sit back, relax and stay a while.

Ale House

33 Main St., Amesbury, MA (978) 388-1950

www.amesburyalehouse.com

The Ale House in downtown Amesbury is a family friendly restaurant in a beautiful brick building on the banks of the Pow Wow River. You'll find a festive bar area, busy dining room and comfortable leather couches. With twenty-four taps and about a hundred bottles, you know they're serious about beer. As for the food, there's steak frites with melted blue cheese and caramelized onions, fresh jalapenos stuffed with bacon and cheese, lobster sliders, Patty Melts and the ultimate in drinking food: poutine. Of course, nothing goes better with beer than pizza, and you've never tasted anything like the Ale House Special, which has a pesto base topped with fried salami and mozzarella.

Cape Ann Brewing Company

11 Rogers St., Gloucester, MA (978) 282-7399

www.capeannbrewing.com

Part restaurant, part brewery and part German-style beer hall, the Cape Ann Brewing Company has quickly become THE place for food and beer lovers on the North Shore. Situated right on Gloucester Harbor, there are festive wooden picnic tables inside and out on the oceanfront deck. All the beer is brewed in house and blended into various menu items. The barbecue sauce is made with the Honey Pilsner. The Fisherman's Brew is used in the bratwurst. Mussels are steamed to perfection in Bavarian Wheat. They even infuse their house made mozzarella with Cape Ann's flagship Fisherman's Ale.

Watch City Brewing Co.

256 Moody St., Waltham, MA (781) 647-4000

www.watchcitybrew.com

Since 1996, the Watch City Brewing Company has been the place to get what you crave, both on the plate and in the glass. This big, casual restaurant is typically full of friendly beer snobs looking for the next best brew. Watch City serves tasty beers like the Moody Street Stout or the Hops Explosion IPA, as they rotate more seasonal beers like the Pumpkin-Eye Pumpkin Ale. All the food at Watch City is beer friendly and wallet friendly. There's Ale Battered Fish & Chips, Watch City Meatloaf and tender steak frites for under twenty bucks. Beef, turkey and lamb burgers are big, weighing in at a half pound with loads of toppings to add on. True diehards join Watch City's mug club, which offers members exclusive benefits including their own mug for use at the brewery.

Breakfast
GREAT ATE

Amber Road Cafe

635 Washington St., Canton, MA (339) 237-3925

www.amberroadcafe.net

Situated in Downtown Canton, this bright, cheery breakfast and lunch spot is a casual dining experience with inspirational messages on the walls and lines out the door. The Amber Omelette is overloaded with smoked bacon, melted cheese, baby spinach and tomatoes. French Toast is like nothing you've ever seen, stuffed with brie and topped with apple cranberry walnut chutney. The fluffy buttermilk pancakes with caramelized bananas are a must order. On the lunch side of the menu, Amber Road offers a variety of salads and sandwiches coming in both wrap and panini form.

Zaftigs

335 Harvard St., Brookline, MA (617) 975-0075

1298 Worcester Rd., Natick, MA (508) 653-4442

www.zaftigs.com

Zaftigs in Coolidge Corner and Natick is not your father's deli. This modern version of a classic Jewish deli is a triple threat, serving breakfast, lunch and dinner. No matter what you like, they're bound to have it as there are over 250 dishes on the menu. Whether you belly up to the counter or cozy in at a booth, you'll want to try some of Zaftig's potato pancakes. These crispy disks can be stacked and smothered with bacon, cheddar and tomatoes, or served straight up accompanied by sour cream and homemade applesauce. The Banana-Stuffed French Toast has a crunchy exterior and a smooth, sweet finish. For a hearty sandwich, the Meatloaf Melt is a huge chunk of meat popped on a bulkie with spicy Cajun ketchup and plenty of cheddar cheese.

Friendly Toast

1 Kendall Sq., Cambridge, MA (617) 621-1200

113 Congress St., Portsmouth, NH (603) 430-2154

www.thefriendlytoast.net

The Friendly Toast is a one of a kind eatery with a wacky, nostalgic décor, crazy artwork and ultra-creative menu. The Drunkard's French Toast is topped with Grand Marnier and raspberry sauce. The Almond Joy Pancakes are loaded with coconut, almonds and chocolate chips. For something truly over the top, the King Cakes are two pancakes filled with bananas, chocolate chips and peanut butter topped with bacon and whipped cream. While the breakfast menu truly shines, the lunch menu is not to be overlooked as it's lined with a variety of special sandwiches and overstuffed burritos.

Kristin's

349 Washington St., Braintree, MA (781) 843-2022

www.kristinsbraintree.com

Kristin's is an old school spot with an old fashioned counter and a quaint dining room that serves mouthwatering plates from the morning to mid-afternoon. The meaty house made corned beef hash is some of the best Phantom has sampled. There are twenty-five varieties of pancakes from blueberry to German chocolate to the "Birthday Pancake" topped with frosting, sprinkles and a candle. Each can be ordered as a stack or individually so you can sample a few flavors. As for lunch, you have to lay your lips on Kristin's Turkey Club, a colossal sandwich stacked with layers of real homestyle turkey that's roasted every day on-site.

James' Breakfast and More

850 Franklin St., Wrentham, MA (508) 384-0017

www.jamesbreakfastandmore.com

James' Breakfast and More is a family friendly spot that serves impressive breakfast fare, especially for the suburbs. Eggs Benedict is turned on its head, topped with grilled tomato, coconut crab cakes, and homemade dill hollandaise. French Toast is made from thick, fresh baked cinnamon bread topped with fruit and whipped cream. Nothing is as filling as the Cast Iron Killer: a hot skillet filled with home fries, peppers, onions, Jamaican jerk seasoning, a mound of house made hash and a few butter fried eggs. The BLT at James' is more than just bacon, lettuce and tomato. Order the BLOAT and you'll get a super sandwich stacked with bacon, lettuce, onion, avocado and tomato.

Gingerbread Construction Company

562 Washington St., Winchester, MA (781) 729-7700

52 Main St., Wakefield, MA (781) 246-2200

www.gingerbreadusa.com

The Gingerbread Construction Company is a playful spot known for their custom-made gingerbread houses. If you can score one of their few seats, try one of the deliciously decadent muffins. Their nineteen innovative flavors include Boston Kreme, Gingerbread with cream cheese icing and Chocolate Raspberry topped with chocolate flakes and chocolate icing. The Strawberry Shortcake muffin is a summer specialty, enveloping ripe fruit and whipped cream. Phantom's absolute favorite is the Chocolate Dreme, made by injecting a moist chocolate muffin with luscious chocolate cream. These muffins are bigger than most with tops much larger than the base.

Mul's Diner

75 West Broadway, Boston, MA (617) 268-5748

It may not look like much from the outside, but this no frills Southie mainstay serves some seriously tasty food. The entire Mul's menu lists old school breakfast favorites. There's Eggs Benedict layered with Prime New York sirloin. Corned beef hash is made with perfectly seasoned brisket. For a bit of breakfast AND dessert, Phantom loves the Crème Brulee French Toast. It's an infusion of sorts, with a thick piece of French Toast slathered with cream, sprinkled with sugar and torched like the classic French dessert.

In a Pickle

655 Main St., Waltham, MA (781) 891-1212

www.in-a-pickle.com

In a Pickle is about the quirkiest way you could start your day, with bright green walls and a silly pickle logo. This greasy spoon will bring out the kid in you with every bite of their absolutely enormous flapjacks. These fluffy buttermilk pancakes can be loaded with Snickers, M&Ms or Reese's Peanut Butter Cups. There are over a dozen creative omelettes like the El Diablo filled with diced onions, bell peppers, tomatoes, jalapenos, melted cheddar and a lime Buffalo hot sauce. There are also plenty of breakfast sandwiches and burritos served right through lunchtime.

Brunch
GREAT ATE

Henrietta's Table

1 Bennett St., Cambridge, MA (617) 661-5005

www.henriettastable.com

Henrietta's Table in the Charles Hotel is an expansive, country style dining room with oversized cupboards, wood floors, harvest photos and rustic linens. The spotless brunch setup displays islands of tiered food and huge cast iron pots along a lengthy kitchen counter. The Sunday brunch buffet is a self-serve, all-you-can-eat, gluttonous feast of locally farmed fruits, grilled veggies, salads, shucked oysters, seafood, seven kinds of pate, cheeses, eggs, hot entrees, roasts, waffles, pastry and dessert. Whether you're looking to impress the boss, the in-laws or just fill your belly, Henrietta's is a no-brainer.

Blue Inc.

131 Broad St., Boston, MA (617) 261-5353

www.blueincboston.com

The brainchild of Hell's Kitchen contestant Jason Santos, Blue Inc. serves some of Boston's most inventive food like mini Kobe corn dogs, duck fat waffle fries with smoked Gouda and hoisin glazed duck confit with cashews. Not to be outdone, the drink menu takes creativity to the next level with cocktails containing fire-roasted marshmallows and nitrogen infused foams. The "Superhero Brunch" on Sundays features servers dressed in comic book costumes delivering dishes like the Superman: a hearty portion of eggs, cheese, waffle fries, bacon and sausage gravy. Creative cocktails are also featured at brunch, like the Kryptonians Delight (Tanqueray, Green Chartreuse, mint and lime).

Tremont 647

647 Tremont St., Boston, MA (617) 266-4600

www.tremont647.com

Tremont 647 is known for its unusually delicious food, and every Saturday and Sunday the stylish space transforms into a wicked fun pajama brunch. Customers and servers roll out of bed and sport their sleepwear right into the dining room. The daring menu dishes out pepper rimmed Bloody Marys with pickled green beans, the Breakfast Crab Rangoon Scramble, Fried Chicken "Benedict" and

Vanilla Rhubarb Baked French Toast. Some servers have been known to get a little risqué with their bedtime attire, and there have even been reports of a certain caped critic sporting purple silk PJs.

SoundBites

704 Broadway Ball Sq., MA (617) 623-8338

www.soundbitesrestaurant.com

SoundBites may have pushy service, long lines and a "no newspapers" rule, but Phantom can't resist their Belgian waffles. Traditional or multi-grain squares are topped with whipped cream and a mountain of exotic fresh fruit like papaya, kiwi, banana and mango. Additional standouts include grilled blueberry muffins, the "Art, Tom & Jack" omelette filled with artichokes, tomatoes and jack cheese, and the "No Place Like Home Fries", which are essentially a block of mashed potatoes with a crunchy exterior. While waiting for a table, customers can get started at the self-service coffee bar.

Masa

439 Tremont St., Boston, MA (617) 338-8884

350 Cambridge Rd., Woburn, MA (781) 938-8886

www.masarestaurant.com

Masa is the exception to the rule in the swank South End, offering bargain food and a hot, spicy scene. The copper bar is inviting for cocktails, and you can score $1 Southwest tapas during set times depending upon the day. The brunch menu begins with a lineup of liquor. There's the superbly made Bloody Masa with top of the line tequila, and the Latin Bellini with Champagne and a mango/guava puree. Sweet brunch plates include Jalisco Chocolate Chip Pancakes or the Nut Crusted Texas Toast stuffed with caramelized bananas. Phantom can't resist the Huevos Rancheros with queso cotija, salsa ranchero, crisp tortillas and black beans.

Julian's

318 Broadway, Providence, RI (401) 861-1770

www.juliansprovidence.com

Julian's is a vintage bistro with starving-artist style that captures the softer side of punk. The exposed brick space brings together a huge disco ball, LEGO art and a brass cappuccino machine that won't quit. Julian's is open for brunch every day at 9am and serves seven versions of hash, like mushroom and Boursin or duck confit. Twenty-eight omelette toppings make the menu, along with seven kinds of Eggs Benedict like the Desperado with avocado and salsa. There's a huge list of pancakes with nuts, chocolate and fruit that can be cooked in the batter or added on top. All of Julian's brunch items can be kicked up a notch by ordering one of six different mimosas.

Aquitaine

569 Tremont St., Boston, MA (617) 424-8577

11 Boylston St., Chestnut Hill, MA (617) 734-8400

500 Legacy Place, Dedham, MA (781) 471-5212

www.aquitaineboston.com

Aquitaine is the perfect place for a first date or a filling brunch. They're known for hearty portions of classic French dishes for dinner, but Phantom prefers the brunch experience on Saturday and Sunday. Die-hards die for the French Toast: two golden-brown slices of brioche with crispy bacon, homemade whipped cream and fresh berries in a sweet coating of maple syrup. Ample omelettes have French touches like the Basquaise with gruyere, ham and parsley. There's even a prix fixe brunch menu offering a cinnamon bun, choice of omelette, potatoes, fresh orange juice and coffee for less than ten bucks a person.

Bullfinchs

730 Boston Post Rd., Sudbury, MA (978) 443-4094

www.bullfinchs.com

Bullfinchs brings brunch you'd normally find in the city to MetroWest. This cozy eatery has been making elegant brunches served along with live jazz for thirty years. Phantom's favorite part of the meal comes in the beginning with a complimentary basket full fresh baked muffins, scones and Bullfinchs' signature coffee cake. As tempting as that basket may be, it pales in comparison to Bullfinchs' luscious Lobster Benedict or the absolutely beautiful Texas-style French Toast. Two colossal pieces of Texas toast are dipped in a custard batter, rolled in Panko bread crumbs, pan fried golden brown and sprinkled with cinnamon and sugar.

Buffets/Big Portions

GREAT ATE

Nordic Lodge

178 East Pasquiset Trail, Charlestown, RI (401) 783-4515

www.nordiclodge.com

The Nordic Lodge is the biggest and tastiest buffet you can find outside of Las Vegas, featuring over 100 top quality items from soup to nuts, oysters to ice cream sundaes. The biggest draw is the all you can eat lobster. They serve up to 3,500 pounds of lobster a day along with 150 pounds of butter and over 1,000 pounds of fresh Alaskan crab. There's also a massive dessert table and an entire Haagen-Dazs ice cream sundae bar. Diners have two hours to feast on as much as they can. The food is only part of the attraction because the property has plenty of room to roam when you're done eating with three lakes, fire pits, hammocks, live animals and outdoor music. Open April to December, a trip to the buffet runs around $85 per person including tax, tip and soft drinks.

Carl's Oxford Diner

291 Main St., Oxford, MA (508) 987-8770

Carl's Oxford Diner serves everything in one size: large. There are five egg omelettes, thick cut ham and "sides" of bacon boasting ten slices. Some breakfast favorites include a double stacked strawberry waffle and the steak and cheese omelette that's overloaded with meat. Carl's looks like a typical greasy spoon, with a counter full of regulars sucking back OJ out of plastic cups. Phantom's favorite dish, the "Bacon Special", is a monster of a meal with lots of bacon, three eggs and a mound of homefries. With meals like steak tips and eggs coming in south of ten bucks, you won't break the bank on breakfast.

Buca di Beppo

233 Elm St., Dedham, MA (781) 329-2502

7 Boston Tpke., Shrewsbury, MA (508) 792-1737

www.bucadibeppo.com

This national chain serves portions so big, they require an oversized spoon for serving. The atmosphere is always festive with a big open kitchen, thousands of pictures on the walls and a private dining room paying homage to the Pope. The portions come family style, so a small is good enough for two people and a large can feed about six. Pastas are presented in bowls so big you could practically dive right in, like the spaghetti served with meatballs that weigh half-a-pound each and baked rigatoni packed with sausage and cheese. The nine layer lasagna measures twelve inches long, four inches high, and four inches wide. If you can somehow make it to dessert, you might as well go all the way and order the Colossal Brownie Sundae served in a giant martini glass.

Midwest Grill

1124 Cambridge St., Cambridge, MA (617) 354-7536

910 Broadway, Saugus, MA (781) 231-2221

www.midwestgrillrestaurant.com

The Midwest Grill is an energetic, authentic Brazilian churrascaria that's part buffet, part barbecue and part steak house. They offer a huge range of meats like steak, pork loin, chicken, lamb, beef ribs, pork ribs and two types of sausage. They're all cooked to perfection and served on massive skewers circulated throughout the dining room and sliced to order right at the table. The skewers don't stop until you flash a two-sided card from green to red when you've had enough. Plus, there's a full buffet packed with endless amounts of rice and beans, fried plantains and fresh veggies. But let's be honest, nobody comes for the salad!

Minado

1282 Worcester Rd., Natick, MA (508) 647-0495

www.minado.com

Phantom is skeptical whenever he see the words "sushi" and "buffet" in the same sentence. However, Minado's all-you-can-eat feast is expansive without compromising quality. The cavernous 360 seat dining room invites seafood lovers to sink their teeth into 100 selections of maki, sashimi, and hand rolls. Along with tuna, eel, and yellow tail, there's crab with avocado, fried salmon, and shrimp tempura. Freshness is guaranteed, with no piece sitting out more than fifteen minutes. The friendly staff is sometimes slow to restock the lobster tail and crab legs, but they're worth the wait.

Eagles Deli

1918 Beacon St., Brighton, MA (617) 731-3232

www.eaglesdeli.com

Eagles Deli in in Cleveland Circle is a quick-service, order-at-the-counter burger joint packed with Boston College students digging into ludicrously large plates of cheap grub. The no-nonsense space is decked out in faux picnic tables, exposed ducts and photos of triumphant members of the Clean Plate Club. Eagles is home to an insane eating challenge named after a regular with a mammoth appetite: the "Reilly Burger". This serious stacking of six half-pound patties is topped with twelve slices of cheese held together by a wooden teriyaki stick. It comes with five pounds of fries and unlimited fountain soda to wash it all down.

Wright's Farm

200 Woonsocket Hill Rd., North Smithfield, RI (401) 767-3014

www.wrightsdairyfarm.com

Wright's Farm is a sprawling poultry-gorging paradise. The décor dates back to 1970, but the multiple rooms of folks dining family-style have a timeless charm. Ordering doesn't come any easier. Everyone gets the same thing: all-you-can-eat platters of roast chicken and sides, with a steak option for hardcore carnivores. For sides, Phantom loves Wright's hand cut French fries with a little malt vinegar. An ice cream disk with a chicken-shaped chocolate center is the only dessert. If that isn't enough, you can satisfy your sweet tooth with candy from their gift shop.

Causeway Restaurant

78 Essex Ave., Gloucester, MA (978) 281-5256

The Causeway is a no frills BYOB restaurant that's been serving ridiculous portions of comfort food for nearly a decade. Eye-popping specialties include the seafood marinara so large it's served in a wok. The Surf and Turf is a delicious duo of baked sirloin and shrimp casserole. The Causeway's most famous dish is the gigantic, overflowing bowl of homemade fish chowder. It's absolutely packed with flavor and close to a pound of fresh seafood. Since it's connected to a liquor store, you don't have to go too far to get your beverages.

Burgers
GREAT ATE

Fuddruckers

50 Walkers Brook Dr., Reading, MA (781) 942-4891

550 Turnpike St., North Andover, MA (978) 557-1100

900 Broadway, Saugus, MA (781) 233-6399

Village Mall, 436 Broadway, Methuen, MA (978) 685-9300

www.fuddruckers.com

Fuddruckers is a fantastically fun burger chain, perfect for all ages with counter service and a buzzing dining room. The hand-packed patties come in four sizes that reach up to an entire pound. But, size doesn't matter because the all-you-can-top produce bar is what makes this place special, loaded with everything from lettuce, tomato and onion to nacho cheese, pico de gallo and jalapenos. Smoked bacon, homemade chili and guacamole cost a little extra. The house baked buns are fluffy, buttery and soak up the juice dripping from your burger. There are also extra thick shakes in flavors like Oreo, coffee or mocha.

R.F. O'Sullivan's Pub

282 Beacon St., Somerville, MA (617) 492-7773

www.rf-osullivan.com

R.F. O'Sullivan's Pub is a small spot with a rectangular bar at the center. Phantom loves this place for thick, juicy, mouthwatering burgers at their jaw-breaking best. Each belly-busting beast is a half-pound of ground sirloin that requires twenty minutes on the grill. O'Sullivan's is also one of the only restaurants that will actually serve a burger the way Phantom likes it: RARE! The menu lists more than two dozen burgers like the Black and Blue coated in fresh ground black pepper and blue cheese. There's also the Chinatown burger doused in teriyaki. The French Dip is topped with sauteed onions and cheese. Be sure to order some of their famous oversized steak fries on the side.

Wahlburgers

19 Shipyard Dr., Hingham, MA (781) 749-2110

www.wahlburgers.com

The hottest new burger joint this side of Hollywood, Wahlburgers is the latest creation of chef Paul Wahlberg and his famous actor brothers Mark and Donnie. Located in the Hingham Shipyard across the street from sister restaurant Alma Nove, Wahlburgers has two dining options: either quick counter service or sit down dining. The three ounce all-natural burgers are griddled on the flat-top and served with lettuce, tomato and house made pickles on a fresh baked roll. Beyond beef, there's also a salmon burger and the ground turkey Thanksgiving Burger topped with stuffing, orange cranberry sauce, butternut squash and mayo. Phantom also recommends the creamy frappes, sweet potato tots and the "Stray Dog", topped with mustard, sriracha sauce and house smoked tomato salsa.

Back Bay Social Club

867 Boylston St., Boston, MA (617) 247-3200

www.backbaysocialclub.com

Casual with a busy post work crowd, the Back Bay Social Club is a comfortable two floor restaurant with a prime location. In an upscale neighborhood like this, the burger is appropriately gourmet. Ten ounces of perfectly cooked prime beef is topped with extra sharp cheddar cheese and slow cooked sweet onions. Phantom calls this burger an affordable luxury because the price tag for all this hand-held deliciousness, with a side of golden hand cut fries, is over twenty-two dollars (and worth every cent). Beyond the burger, a must try is the Social Club's "Meat Candy". Served in a crock, this sliced kielbasa glazed with pineapple and brown sugar is awesomely addictive.

Mr. Bartley's Gourmet Burgers

1246 Massachusetts Ave., Cambridge, MA (617) 354-6559

www.mrbartley.com

Bartley's is nearly part of the Harvard curriculum, with dorm-like décor and modest plastic patio seating. Their incredible hamburger selection includes dozens of cleverly named creations. The Viagra Burger rises to the occasion with blue cheese and bacon, while the People's Republic of Cambridge is liberally topped with coleslaw and Russian dressing. The Tom Brady is an all-star burger with cheddar, guacamole, and red onions and the Jersey Shore is topped with bacon, grilled mushrooms, onions and of course, plenty of cheese. Sweet potato fries and a Peppermint Patty frappe are must tries.

Boston Burger Company

37 Davis Sq., Somerville, MA (617) 440-7361

1100 Boylston St., Boston, MA (857) 233-4560

www.bostonburgerco.com

The Boston Burger Company is a casual burger joint where you can throw down some beers with some of the most creative burgers you've ever tasted. They put almost anything on a burger, from hellishly hot habanero salsa, to peanut butter, bacon and fried bananas. In fact, there are two dozen specialty burgers, like The Mac Attack topped with homemade mac and cheese and bacon, the Killer Bee super stacked with beer battered onion rings dripping with honey barbecue sauce, and the Hot Mess loaded with 1000 Island dressing and sweet potato fries. Every burger comes with a side of addictive homemade potato chips, or you can upgrade to the BBC sweet potato fries smothered in cinnamon and caramel.

Tasty Burger

1301 Boylston St., Boston, MA (617) 425-4444

69 L St., South Boston, MA (617) 425-4444

www.tastyburger.com

Tasty Burger is a California style burger joint located just steps away from Fenway Park. They serve juicy charbroiled patties, crispy onion strings, and thick creamy milkshakes. Burgers go from the basic double cheese, to the inventive Double Onion topped with sweet caramelized onions and golden onion strings, to absolutely insane creations like the batter fried Blue Collar burger with honey mustard. The top selling burger is the Big Kahuna with grilled pineapple, grilled red onion, and house made teriyaki sauce. For a mindblowing burger experience, Phantom reccomends the super sinful Butta Burger topped with a heaping scoop of fresh whipped butter. Nothing goes better with a burger than a can of craft beer, a refreshing lime-mint slushie or a rich mint chocolate chip milkshake.

Harry's Bar & Burger

121 North Main St., Providence, RI (401) 228-7437

www.harrysbarburger.com

Harry's Bar & Burger is a casual, kitschy eatery with cow statues outside to greet you and a cowhide pattern on the walls. The menu kicks it old school by serving sliders. These mini burger burgers may be small, but they're big on flavor and always come in orders of two. Made with premium beef and topped with finely diced onions, the patties are cooked on a flat top until they form a delicious crust. Each one is served on a toasted buttered potato roll. Sliders can also come stacked with toppings, like the Pig Pile featuring barbecued pulled pork or the

Crunch Burger finished with tangy, spicy haystack onion strings. To wash it all down, there are fifty beers and hard shakes like the Bourbon Brownie, blending ice cream, brownies, Frangelico and Kentucky bourbon.

Chinese
GREAT ATE

Mai Place

323 Turnpike St., Canton, MA (781) 828-1200

Mai Place is a combination sushi bar and Chinese restaurant, serving Asian delights with the care, quality and style you don't often find outside the city. The boneless ribs are sweet and tender. The pineapple fried rice can be baked in the shell so every grain is infused with extra flavor. If you want to triple your Mai Place experience, try the Triple Delights in a Crispy Nest. Shrimp, beef, chicken and plenty of mixed vegetables are tossed in a tangy sauce and served in a nest made of fried potato sticks, so once you finish the filling, you can eat the bowl, too.

Quan's Kitchen

871 Washington St., Hanover, MA (781) 826-8868

652 East Washington St., North Attleboro, MA (508) 699-7826

www.quanskitchen.net

From the outside, Quan's in Hanover looks like a palace. Inside, you'll find a massive space decked out with artifacts, statues and stylish lighting. The Pu Pu Platter is presented on porcelain, but it's filled with so many appetizing options, you can barely see the platter underneath. There are crispy chicken wings, tender beef teriyaki, golden fried shrimp, plump egg rolls, and an ample stack of sticky-sweet boneless spare ribs. There's sushi like the Lobster Tempura maki sliced and diced right in front of you. Quan's Steak features marinated slices of top quality Hong Kong style beef pan-seared and plated with sweet peppers and onions in a luxurious black pepper sauce. Quan's also has takeout spots in Mansfield and Weymouth.

Red Lantern

39 Stanhope St., Boston, MA (617) 262-3900

www.redlanternboston.com

Red Lantern in the Back Bay is a sexy space that's part upscale Asian restaurant and part swanky night club. Scantily clad servers bring out giant scorpion bowls as an open kitchen of screaming hot woks cooks everything from Chinese style

"Broken Lobster" to the tender teriyaki noodle steak. There's a full list of creative sushi and steaks like the Chinese tenderloin that's wrapped in bacon and served with lobster whipped potatoes. Elaborately decorated with nine foot Buddhas and dim lighting, this restaurant is great for large groups. There's a private dining room for more intimate celebrations.

Myers + Chang

1145 Washington St., Boston, MA (617) 542-5200

www.myersandchang.com

Myers + Chang in the South End is a kitschy pan-Asian greasy spoon with an urban-hipster edge. They offer a mix of Chinese, Taiwanese, Thai and Vietnamese dishes that are priced reasonably for the South End. Appetizers include Mama Chang's Pork and Chive Dumplings and wok roasted mussels served with grilled garlic toast. Entrees like the tea smoked pork ribs are amazingly tender. There are also several special menus that cater to vegetarians and gluten or nut free diets. While there isn't a dessert menu, Myers + Chang offers a complimentary sweet to round out your meal.

Lavender

519 A Boston Post Rd., Sudbury, MA (978) 579-9988

www.lavenderasiancuisine.com

At Lavender, they serve fresh, affordable cuisine in an upscale setting. Lobster lovers have many tempting offers including the addictive lobster lettuce wraps served with a tangy hoisin sauce or the twin lobster tails fired in a wok with ginger and scallions. For something a little sweeter, there's the light and flavorful pineapple fried rice and tropical pineapple chicken served right in the shell. Lavender's generous scorpion bowls are a popular attraction at the sleek martini bar. Live karaoke on Thursday, Friday and Saturday might be fun, but it's loud, so finish your meal before 9pm.

Golden Temple

1651 Beacon St., Brookline, MA (617) 277-9722

www.healthyfreshfood.com

Where else can you get fine Chinese food while putting back the strongest Mai Tais on the eastern seaboard? "The Temple" is one of the most beautiful Chinese restaurants in New England, with a modern mix of architecture, lighting and music. The high-end cuisine comes at a price, but luxurious dishes like the

Chardonnay Chicken and batter-fried lobster are worth a few extra bucks. Phantom suggests the special cut Golden Temple Ribs, which have a cult-like following. This Brookline institution is always innovating, and the bar scene sizzles at night with a house DJ and dancing.

All Seasons Table

64 Pleasant St., Malden, MA (781) 397-8788

www.allseasonstablerestaurant.com

All Seasons Table is a beautifully modern Pan-Asian eatery that you definitely wouldn't expect to find in Malden Center. The space is minimally decorated with a long, active bar serving both booze and an extensive list of sushi. The menu spans from Thai dishes like the Drunken Noodles or Fresh King Crab Thai Style to Chinese classics like Peking Duck and General Gao's Chicken. The appetizer sampler has all the hits, including teriyaki, boneless ribs, chicken wings and the top Phan favorite: Crab Rangoon. Cocktails are stiff and can be enjoyed with live jazz on the weekends.

Great Chow

17 Beale St., Quincy, MA (617) 328-1338

497 Bedford St., Abington, MA (781) 871-8832

www.great-chow.com

The folks at Great Chow love to shake things up with colorful cocktails, creative sushi, and tempting appetizers laid out in a world-class Pu Pu Platter. People come from near and far to feast on Pan Asian fare like Pad Thai, Szechuan Spicy Beef and boats of sushi for sharing. The sleek dining room houses an elegant slow motion waterfall. The lounge is always active with a boisterous crowd, huge TVs and live dance music on the weekends. Both locations offer takeout and delivery if you want to enjoy all that great chow from the comfort of your home.

Chocolate
GREAT ATE

Max Brenner

745 Boylston St., Boston, MA (617) 274-1741

www.maxbrenner.com

You'll feel like a kid in a candy store when you walk into this sit down restaurant/ lab with beakers lining the walls and chocolate served in syringes. The sign on the door reads "Chocolate by the Bald Man". That bald man, Max Brenner, is constantly experimenting with new ways to break the chocolate mold. The menu is lined with everything from double chocolate pancakes to chocolate fondue with ice cream popsicle dippers. There are even savory chocolate items from the dinner menu like Brenner's black and tan beer battered onion rings with dark chocolate ranch dressing, perfect when washed down with a creative chocolate inspired cocktail.

Amy's Apples

128 Pleasant View Ave., Smithfield, RI (401) 233-2000

www.amysapples.com

Amy's Apples is a small candy shop with big flavors and even bigger apples. These larger than life fruit on a stick are dipped in chocolate and topped with everything from cookies and candy to raisins and nuts. There's the Oreo Cookie Madness layered with crumbles of everyone's favorite cookie and the luxurious White Chocolate Cranberry Chip. The Black Forest Apple is sinful, covered with dark chocolate chips and drizzled with white chocolate and sundried cherries. Phantom is pretty partial to the decadent Triple Chocolate Divinity that's covered with milk chocolate, dark chocolate chips and topped with white chocolate. These sweets are a perfect gift and can be ordered and shipped nationwide.

Hilliard's House of Candy

95 Washington St., Canton, MA (781) 828-9004

316 Main St., North Easton, MA (508) 238-6231

122 Webster St., Hanover, MA (781) 878-8533

www.hilliardscandy.com

Hilliard's House of Candy has been an institution of all things sweet since 1924. They have everything chocolate under one roof including truffles, premium fudge, barks, brittles, chocolate dipped fruit, and their famous Almond Toffee Crunch. There are varieties of mixed nuts like the "Movie Mix" with butter toasted peanuts, BBQ corn sticks, mini pretzels, cheddar crackers, sesame sticks and honey roast sesame chips. There's even a line of sugar free chocolates for folks with diet restrictions.

Yummies

384 U.S. Rte. 1, Kittery, ME (207) 439-9156

www.yummies.com

Yummies on Route One is a candy store like no other. Over 10,000 pounds of candy and nuts are on display from floor to ceiling, front to back, wall to wall, side to side. An entire wall is dedicated to chocolate covered items. Another displays every Pez dispenser currently in production. What truly sets Yummies apart is their large selection of old fashioned and hard to find candies. If you're looking for Bit-O-Honey, Turkish Taffy, Candy Buttons, or Mary Janes, Yummies has them all. You can even get the "Retro Candy Gift Box" for a nostalgic collection of sweets from the 50's, 60's, 70's and 80's.

The Chocolate Truffle

18 Thompson St., Winchester, MA (781) 729-0409

494 Main St., Reading, MA (781) 944-7155

www.thechocolatetruffle.com

Chocoholics be warned. This is the ultimate chocolate shop. The Chocolate Truffle has an enormous selection of sweet treats like you've never seen. They make jumbo sized peanut butter cups with crazy flavors like M&M, marshmallow or chocolate chip. There's a PB&J truffle that will bring you back to when you enjoyed the classic sandwich as a kid. The lumpy, bumpy dessert pizza is made of milk chocolate and topped with cookie crumbles, white chocolate, Heath Bar, pretzels and M&Ms. They even coat everything from Twinkies to Pringles in their rich, luxuriant chocolate.

The Citizen

120 Commercial St., Worcester, MA (508) 459-9090

www.thecitizenwinebar.com

The Citizen is a fun, lively restaurant that takes chocolate seriously. The menu is divided into sections of wine, cheese and chocolate. Customers choose from each group to create their own tasting platters served on wooden boards. There are more than a dozen cheeses nightly and every board comes with fresh honeycomb, house made fig paste and plenty of French bread. The wine and chocolates work the same way. You can customize a tasting of dark, milk and white chocolates from around the world. Every bottle of wine is available in a three ounce pour, so you can always sample something different.

L.A. Burdick Chocolate

52 Brattle St., Cambridge, MA (617) 491-4340

220 Clarendon St., Boston, MA (617) 303-0113

47 Main St., Walpole, NH (603) 756-2882

www.burdickchocolate.com

Burdick Chocolate is a cozy European style cafe turning out the most delicious chocolate treats. Their hot chocolate is hands down the best Phantom has ever tasted. Poured into a giant mug, this rich drink is like a liquefied candy bar mixed with steamed milk. Their adorable chocolate mice are almost too cute to eat, constructed with a ganache body, almond ears, and a ribbon tail. Other treats include dessert cakes, fruit tartlets, and tea cookies. Burdick's flagship location is in Walpole, NH.

Turtle Alley

177 Essex St., Salem, MA (978) 740-0660

42 Rogers St., Gloucester, MA (978) 281-4000

www.turtlealley.com

Turtle Alley is a sweet shop that creates some of the finest, freshest handmade chocolates in New England. Whether you go for their fudge, toffee or truffles, you're sure to spike your sugar level . The one thing you have to try at Turtle Alley is their signature caramel packed turtles. Available in dark, milk and white chocolate, each one of these craveable clusters is produced on-site and packed with fresh roasted nuts. They also offer all your favorite penny candies from yesteryear like Swedish Fish, Gummi Worms and Sour Patch Kids.

Comfort Food
GREAT ATE

Harrows Chicken Pie

126 Main St., Reading, MA (781) 944-0410

275 Mystic Ave., Medford, MA (781) 306-0410

352 Broadway, Saugus, MA (781) 231-7410

345 Main St., Tewksbury, MA (978) 858-0411

www.chickenpie.com

Harrows in Reading has served their world famous chicken pies for over seventy years. These hand-crafted chicken pies are filled with slow-roasted chicken, homestyle gravy, potatoes and carrots baked in a buttery, flaky crust. Whichever location you visit, you can buy their pies cold to heat up at home, or call ahead to have a piping hot pie ready for pickup. Plus, this convenient takeout operation offers creamy mashed potatoes, fresh-baked blueberry pie and soft dinner rolls perfect for ripping, dipping and mopping up every last drop of chicken pie.

Cotton

75 Arms St., Manchester, NH (603) 622-5488

www.cottonfood.com

Cotton is a hip and happening restaurant featuring high ceilings and cool candlelight, with a menu full of fresh, hearty, upscale comfort food. Along with Asian potstickers and almond-crusted turkey schnitzel, you'll find wood grilled steaks, banana bread pudding and the ridiculously popular retro meatloaf served with all-you-can-eat mashed potatoes. Cotton pours forty wines by the glass and dozens of martinis at the long, beautiful bar, making it the perfect place to unplug and unwind.

The Fat Cat

24 Chestnut St., Quincy, MA (617) 471-4363

www.fatcatrestaurant.com

The Fat Cat is a cool, comfortable neighborhood restaurant with an industrial feel and affordable American cuisine. The menu is a mix of comfort foods from across the country like the Steak Philly with roasted peppers and caramelized onions or Southern style dill pickles. The Fat Cat's comfort food comes with many options. Fries are available in four different spices: Cajun, blackened, fajita, or garlic and Parmesan. Nachos can be ordered traditional or topped with BBQ pork, lobster, crab or Buffalo chicken. There are eight types of wings and the mac and cheese can be amped up by adding lobster, steak, shrimp, crab or chicken.

Fireplace

1634 Beacon St., Brookline, MA (617) 975-1900

www.fireplacerest.com

The Fireplace offers a cozy, yet stylish space with warm decor, a working fireplace and an open kitchen that casts its stone oven smell over snugly spaced tables. No detail is overlooked, from the copper tabletops and wrought iron lighting to the feel good music of jazz and oldies. The leather-bound and short-winded menu opens up to New England comfort food from the grill with a healthy selection of locally brewed beers and American wines. The signature dish is the all-natural, spit roasted, Maple Glazed Half Chicken served with mashed potatoes and sage brown butter. While the Fireplace is great for an intimate dinner, Phantom likes to take in the trendy, yet cozy atmosphere at the bar with a snack and a fabulous cocktail. Limited parking is behind the restaurant and metered spots line Beacon Street.

The Gallows

1395 Washington St., Boston, MA (617) 425-0200

www.thegallowsboston.com

The Gallows is a cozy, dimly lit spot where South End hipsters line the bar for a cocktail or take in a meal in the dining room. The menu is full of comfort food like bacon caramel popcorn popped in bacon fat and double fried French fries covered in house made gravy and cheese. The Scotch Egg features a deep fried soft boiled egg wrapped in pork sausage. Entrees include hanger steak with creamed spinach and a Carpet Burger stacked with fried oysters and remoulade. The weekend brunch offers a "Tower of Power", stacked with French toast, pulled pork, Canadian bacon, scrambled eggs, country gravy, collard greens and garnishes.

The Local

1391 Washington St., West Newton, MA (617) 340-2160

www.thelocalnewton.com

The Local is a relaxing, casual neighborhood gastropub with a comfort food menu that serves the classics. Potato chips are served warm by the bucket with a side of French Onion dip. There's addictive truffled Parmesan fries and crispy fried pickles that are sliced, deep fried and served with a little spicy mayo. Mac and cheese comes three ways: chicken and bacon, lobster and three cheeses, or truffle oil and chive. The comfort continues on the entrée menu with dishes like fish and chips, lobster rolls, short ribs and steak tips.

Foundry on Elm

255 Elm St., Somerville, MA (617) 628-9999

www.foundryonelm.com

Foundry on Elm is a popular neighborhood eatery with a French brasserie vibe thanks to chandelier lighting, red banquettes and mirror-flanked walls. Patrons drink craft beers at the white marble bar as 80's alt-pop plays overhead. Every item on the sprawling menu is classic comfort food with a twist. Fried calamari and poutine are a great way to start your gorge. There are four flatbreads with gourmet toppings like wild mushrooms and truffle oil or squash blossoms with fresh ricotta. The Parisian gnocchi will stick to your ribs topped with a Parmesan brown butter. For a truly comforting meal on a cold day, the Boeuf Bourguignon is a tasty way to warm up. Lunch is served daily and there's brunch on the weekends. Street parking in Davis Square can be tough but manageable if you circle the block a few times.

Happy's Bar + Kitchen

1363 Boylston St., Boston, MA (857) 753-4100

www.happysbarandkitchen.com

Happy's, near Fenway Park, is a casual, upbeat restaurant with high ceilings and a retro feel. This kitschy, colorful restaurant serves breakfast, lunch and dinner with a full bar to enjoy some post work cocktails. Comfort food is cooked all day with fluffy omelettes in the morning, hot pastrami with Swiss for lunch and boneless fried chicken with spicy honey mango sauce for dinner. Small plates can be enjoyed in the dining room or at the bar with selections like spicy wings, deviled eggs, fried oysters and homemade potato chips. If you want something more than a snack, larger entrees are available like grilled lamb with garlic and old school chicken parm. The restaurant is owned by high end Chef Michael Schlow, but this place is anything but stuffy with graffiti sprayed throughout the urban style dining room.

Cupcakes
GREAT ATE

Cupcake City

137 Main St., Reading, MA (781) 944-0400

www.cupcakecityreading.com

While it may be small in size and to-go only, Cupcake City has treats that are big in flavor. There's the Maple Pancake cupcake topped with a maple syrup brown sugar buttercream and garnished with cinnamon brown sugar and bacon. The Strawberry Shortcake is light and sweet topped with a Swiss strawberry buttercream frosting. There's even a cupcake version of the classic Boston Cream Pie. Private parties can be held in a funky, fun room with a crystal chandelier that hangs overhead. Party attendees get schooled in making fondant for decorating their own box of cupcakes they can take home when all the fun is done.

Crumbs

176 Federal St., Boston, MA (617) 345-9200

Burlington Mall 75 Middlesex Tpke., Burlington, MA (781) 229-6300

www.crumbs.com

One of the original inspirations for the cupcake craze, this national chain has taken Massachusetts by storm. Cupcakes are offered in four sizes, with the largest serving four to six people. The cupcakes come in crazy flavors like Key Lime, Salted Caramel and Red Velvet. The Bababooey cupcake (named after Howard Stern producer, Gary Dell'Abate) features rich chocolate cake covered with peanut butter and chocolate cream cheese, topped with chips and piped full of more peanut butter. There are a few seats, but frequent fliers normally take their cakes to go. New locations are in the Burlington Mall and Natick Mall.

Cakes by Erin

58 Kenoza Ave., Haverhill, MA (978) 469-9136

www.cakesbyerin.com

Cakes by Erin is the brainchild of Erin Erler, who has crafted elaborate event cakes for everyone from Seth MacFarlane to Conan O'Brien. Each over the top confection is customized for you and made meticulously by Erin herself. If you're craving cupcakes, she makes those, too. The always rotating flavors range from Triple Chocolate and Chocolate Chip Cookie Dough to crazier ones like

Margarita, Snickerdoodle and Red Bull & Vodka. There are a few seats to enjoy your sweets and peek into the open kitchen where Erin's confectionary magic happens.

Shotcakes

Burlington Mall, 75 Middlesex Tpke., Burlington, MA (781) 221-2200

www.shot-cakes.com

When a long day of shopping has you famished, Shotcakes in the Burlington Mall food court is the place to be. Besides serving all your frosty favorites like shakes and soft serve, they actually inject cupcakes with ice cream. There are thirty colorful and delicious cupcakes featured every day. Each one is topped with homemade frosting, covered in toppings and most importantly, stuffed with either chocolate or vanilla soft serve using a top secret, patented machine the owner invented himself.

Treat Cupcake Bar

1450 Highland Ave., Needham, MA (781) 444-4995

www.treatcupcakebar.com

The mesmerizing cupcake case at Treat is always packed with amazing creations. There's cafe seating in this bright, colorful eatery with rainbow colored floors. Top sellers include the Needham Cream Pie and Triple Chocolate, featuring chocolate cake, chocolate frosting, and white chocolate filling. If you want a custom cupcake made to your sweet specifications, this is the place to go. Treat is home to an interactive cupcake bar where customers call the shots. You simply grab a seat, pick your favorite flavor of cake, style of frosting, and all kinds of candy toppings, and then you assemble it yourself.

Babycakes

163 Beale St., Quincy, MA (617) 773-4458

www.babycakesshop.net

At Babycakes, it's all cupcakes all the time. Unlike a lot of the trendy cupcake shops out there, these bite sized treats are oversized and underpriced. From Peanut Butter Cup to Strawberry Shortcake to Red Velvet, they're all homemade and incredibly moist, fluffy and delicious. The top treat at Babycakes bares the tiny, takeout shop's name. The Babycake is a chocolate cupcake filled with fresh whipped cream and covered in smooth chocolate ganache with the word "Babycake" scrolled across the top in vanilla icing.

Cupcake Cafe

297 Rantoul St., Beverly (978) 922-9720

Cupcake Cafe takes the cupcake craze to a whole new level. Each one of their sixty flavors will knock your socks off, including the gooey Turtle cupcake sporting a chocolate cake base with chocolate frosting, homemade caramel and pecans. There's a Bananas Foster cupcake packed with sautéed bananas and real whipped cream, and a Snowball cupcake overflowing with marshmallowy pink frosting and shredded coconut. Phantom's favorite is the Fluffernutter, overloaded with marshmallow fluff inside vanilla cake topped with peanut butter cream and chopped peanuts.

Sweet Tooth Boston

371 West Broadway, South Boston, MA (617) 268-2555

www.sweettoothboston.com

Sweet Tooth is the ultimate spot to indulge on over the top cookies, brownies and cupcakes. The "regular" chocolate cupcake is topped with a jumbo sized chocolate dipped strawberry. The Chocolate Truffle cupcake is like two treats in one, with a giant hand dipped truffle on top. For an Asian inspired treat, try the Make-A-Wish cupcake with a chocolate covered fortune cookie crown. Sweet Tooth is a grab-and-go kind of place, where you can also order custom cakes for any kind of celebration.

Desserts
GREAT ATE

Finale

1 Columbus Ave., Boston, MA (617) 423-3184
30 Dunster St., Cambridge, MA (617) 441-9797

www.finaledesserts.com

Defying the mantra of mothers everywhere, Finale insists that dessert comes first. The elegant desserterie serves light meals and hot toddies, but it's the artfully stunning cookies, cakes and chocolates that entice most diners. They're open late for the post theater crowd, perfecting signature dishes like molten chocolate cake and crème brulee. Phantom flips for the Manjari mousse and the tiny little fruit tartlets. Both locations (Boston's Park Plaza and Harvard Square) feature open kitchens where customers can watch as desserts are assembled. Strategically angled mirrors ensure that even the tables at the back of the room get a great view.

Sweet

305 Shrewsbury St., Worcester, MA (508) 373-2248

www.sweetworcester.com

Sweet is a pastry shop with a full bar. The counter in front is fairly traditional with cupcakes and cookies, while the dining room has plenty of tables and a full menu of plated desserts paired with wines, cordials and martinis. Rich chocolate cake is kicked up with chocolate ganache and homemade ice cream. Smooth chocolate fondue is served with homemade marshmallows, graham crackers, fresh fruit and pretzels. The Sweet experience gets even sweeter with a glass of wine that's specifically suggested for every dessert. Phantom loves popping a few of their French donuts back with a nice bubbly glass of champagne. Chef/owner Alina Eisenhauer's looks and skills landed her on a Food Network reality show.

Wicked Whoopies

www.wickedwhoopies.com

Wicked Whoopies is THE authority on making whoopie. Just when you thought the original whoopie pie recipe of whipped cream between devil's food cake couldn't get any better, the folks at Wicked Whoopies have redefined the pie with twenty flavors and variations. Phantom's favorites include strawberry, chocolate chip, and raspberry and cream. There's also a whopping five-pound Jumbo Whoopie and a chocolate dipped "Whoop-de-Doo" that's like a gourmet Ring Ding. They make thousands of pies daily, which you can buy online or in retail stores in Freeport and Farmingdale, Maine.

North End Treats

661 Cochituate Rd., Framingham, MA (508) 620-6836

www.northendtreats.com

This takeout spot offers everything you'd find in the North End. Panini are pressed to order and served hot and crispy. Brick oven pizzas range from traditional pepperoni to gourmet Fig and Prosciutto to Breakfast Pizza with Italian sausage, bacon, mozzarella, and scrambled eggs. North End Treats is serious about sweets like their cannoli and lobster tails that come straight from the North End's famous Bova's Bakery. While the exterior may not have the charm of the old neighborhood, it certainly is a convenient option right off the Mass Pike.

Red Eyed Pig

1753 Centre St., West Roxbury, MA (617) 325-1700

www.red-eyedpig.com

Red Eyed Pig is one of Boston's best new spots for barbecue. This small, mostly takeout spot offers just a few stools to eat in house. The Southern style 'cue is all smoked on-site and includes St. Louis ribs, thick cut brisket and pulled pork finished with Lexington vinegar sauce. The golden hush puppies are served with a sweet orange maple bacon butter and seem more like dessert than a side dish. All of the desserts at the Red Eyed Pig are served in their own personal sized mason jars. There's Apple Crisp, Peanut Butter Pie, Banana Pudding and Mississippi Mud Pie.

Parker's at the Omni Parker House

60 School St., Boston, MA (617) 227-8600

www.omniparkerhouse.com

As the birthplace of the Boston cream pie, Parker's is THE place to order this New England classic. It's not really a pie at all, but a gloriously messy recipe of cushy sponge cake and thick custard topped with chocolate glaze and sliced almonds. Heaping slices are served at the Omni, which is steeped in 19th century history. Politicians and celebrities have long loved the hotel, appointed with bronze, American oak and ostentatious chandeliers. Settling into the over-the-top, extravagant dining room, you'll dine well on local fare like clam chowder and baked Boston scrod.

Pastiche Fine Desserts & Cafe

92 Spruce St., Providence, RI (401) 861-5190

www.pastichefinedesserts.com

Pastiche Fine Desserts is a tantalizing dessert cafe, turning out Phantom's favorite fruit tarts. To make the tarts, they fill a buttery pastry shell with vanilla custard and top it off with concentric circles of jewel-like kiwi, blueberries, strawberries and orange. The space is warm and inviting with small, intimate tables, a working fireplace and sophisticated European character. Pastiche is stocked with other superb sweets like orange chocolate Bavarian cake, Russian teacakes, biscotti, rugelach and chocolate walnut truffle cookies. Beverage options include deluxe coffee concoctions, tea, chai and hot chocolate.

Planet Marshmallow

81 Hanover St., Manchester, NH (603) 625-8111

www.planetmarshmallow.com

Planet Marshmallow is a cool, quirky cafe with exposed brick walls and mellow music piped in from overhead. Homemade marshmallows are the focus, with wacky flavors including Chai Spice, Mint Chocolate Chip, Toasted Coconut and Chocolate Chipotle. Every delicious cube can be bought by the bag on-site or online. These same marshmallows are used on many of the plated desserts including the interactive chocolate fondue and the "S'mores at the Table". This sweet shop does have a savory side with a quiche of the day, chicken salad and a decadent baked brie that's made for sharing.

Diners
GREAT ATE

Dave's Diner

390 West Grove St., Middleboro, MA (508) 923-4755

www.daves-diner.com

Dave's Diner is a throwback restaurant where you can throw down some serious chow. With a jukebox cranking the oldies, classic tile floors, counter stools, vinyl booths and vintage signs, this Middleboro mainstay has the comfort food you crave including breakfast all day. The menu boasts everything from meatloaf sandwiches to malted waffles, chicken parm to chocolate cake, hand-packed burgers to fresh baked blueberry pie. The fried chicken has a cult following, heated in a pressure fryer that cooks at a low temperature, sealing in all the juices so each crispy piece is finger licking good.

Casey's Diner

36 South Ave., Natick, MA (508) 655-3761

Casey's Diner is a Natick institution that's been serving all your favorites for decades. When the door slides open, you'll find yourself back in time to the turn of the century. The space looks like a train car with a few counter stools, a takeout window, and a couple picnic tables to the side. There's a great greasy hamburger cooked on the griddle so it gets a nice crust. The must have menu item at Casey's is the steamed hot dog. Phantom prefers to order his "all around" with mustard, relish and chopped onions. These franks have a large following, and you'll usually find a line going out the door to get them.

Deluxe Station Diner

70 Union St., Newton Centre, MA (617) 244-2550

www.deluxestationdiner.com

The Deluxe Station Diner is a locomotive themed eatery serving diner classics like buttery grilled cheese sandwiches, generous turkey avocado clubs, homestyle mac and cheese and monstrous meatloaf with mashed potatoes. While customers come mostly for the food, the atmosphere is so unique, some people walk in just to take a look around. The building dates back to 1887, with eighteen foot ceilings and original dark wood. Since it's right on the Green line, the "Train Approaching" sign still works. However, these days you can also find neon lights, gears and globes, columns and clocks.

Liberty Elm Diner

777 Elmwood Ave., Providence, RI (401) 467-0777

www.libertyelmdiner.com

This quintessential luncheonette has been a landmark on Elmwood Ave in Providence since 1953. However, there's nothing "greasy" about this spoon. The Liberty Elm uses as many organic ingredients as possible and almost all of it's locally sourced. The cheese and eggs come from Rhode Island. The real maple syrup is the pure, amber goodness from up North. If you're looking for a bit of breakfast, lunch and dinner, the perfect dish to order is the Monte Cristo Sandwich. This sweet and savory stack has thick slices of French toast packed and stacked with melted Swiss and maple baked ham.

Maine Diner

2265 Post Rd., Wells, ME (207) 646-4441

www.mainediner.com

The Maine Diner sticks to tradition, serving huge plates of soulful Yankee fare. There's always a buzz in the dining room complete with both counter and table service. This is probably one of the only places in Maine that doesn't serve full boiled or steamed lobster dinners. They do, however, have lobster quiche, lobster salad, and outstanding lobster rolls. The lobster pie is the best Phantom has ever had, packed with loads of claw and tail meat under a buttery cracker crumb topping. The Lobster Benedict is drenched in Hollandaise sauce and the Lobster club sandwich is a triple-decker of deliciousness piled with bacon, lettuce, tomato and mayo.

Roundabout Diner

580 US Hwy 1 Bypass, Portsmouth, NH (603) 431-1440

www.roundaboutdiner.com

Located right on the Portsmouth Traffic Circle off I-95, the Roundabout Diner is like a new version of the classic '50s diner. There's breakfast all day, like Grand Marnier French Toast made with thick sliced challah bread from When Pigs Fly and a pulled pork omelette bursting with slow smoked meat. Lunch and dinner items include a four cheese mac and cheese packed with sweet Maine lobster, burgers garnished with fried pickles and warm homemade potato chips drenched in blue cheese. With a checkerboard floor, red vinyl chairs, neon signs, and even a full bar, there's plenty to see at the Roundabout. But, nothing catches your attention like the fully stocked pastry case loaded with blueberry pie, banana cream pie and plenty of whoopie pies.

Rox Diner

1881 Centre St., West Roxbury, MA (617) 327-1909

335 Walnut St., Newton, MA (617) 916-1795

www.roxdiner.com

At the Rox Diner, they serve the kind of food you'll want to eat for breakfast, lunch and dinner. French Toast can be stuffed with sweet treats like fresh strawberries and gooey chocolate or crusted in coconut and loaded with juicy mango. The Surf and Turf sliders feature a mini lamb sandwich with cranberry compote along with a bite sized lobster roll. There's a lineup of burgers like the "Lambourgini" topped with pancetta, provolone, arugula and balsamic, as well as plenty of salads, sandwiches and entrees. The newer Newtonville location is a little bigger than the original West Roxbury spot, which can feel cramped at times.

Red Arrow Diner

61 Lowell St., Manchester, NH (603) 626-1118

63 Union Sq., Milford, NH (603) 249-9222

www.redarrowdiner.com

With locations in Milford and Manchester, New Hampshire, the Red Arrow offers all your favorite breakfast, lunch and dinner dishes twenty-four hours a day. Shredded hash browns are cooked on the grill with onions, kielbasa and melted American cheese. The Pastrami Melt will melt in your mouth. A dish of American Chop Suey is comfort food at its finest. However, it's their house made Twinkies or "Dinah Fingers" that keep customers coming back for more. These golden, fluffy cakes are light and airy, filled with sweet vanilla cream cheese frosting.

Family Dining
GREAT ATE

Full Moon

344 Huron Ave., Cambridge, MA (617) 354-6699

www.fullmoonrestaurant.com

Full Moon is a restaurant that caters to adults and children alike. Created by restaurateurs who happened to be mothers of small children, Full Moon has kid friendly fare like hot dogs, French fries, quesadillas, chicken nuggets and ice cream. There's also a more upscale menu for the adults featuring plates like shrimp and avocado salad, roasted chicken with mashed potatoes and grilled trout with basil pesto sauce. While the little ones entertain themselves in a play area, grown-ups can order a beer or a glass of chardonnay. As the evening grows late, Full Moon's demographic turns increasingly more mature, but always full of activity no matter what age you are.

Cabot's

743 Washington St., Newtonville, MA (617) 964-9200

www.cabots.com

Since 1969, this family run, family friendly favorite has served a mind-boggling menu of the coolest treats in town. The Ice Cream Puff puts a scoop of your favorite flavor inside a puff pastry shell topped with hot fudge and whipped cream. The Danielle's Choice sundae is peanut butter cup ice cream smothered with peanut butter fudge, Reese's Pieces and marshmallow. While ice cream may have made Cabot's famous, they're also a full service restaurant serving breakfast all day and fantastic homestyle favorites. The old school atmosphere is thick with nostalgia with seating at booths or along the counter. Visible from the Mass Pike, Cabot's is closed on Monday and accepts cash only, but you won't need much money given super low prices.

Barking Crab

88 Sleeper St., Boston, MA (617) 426-2722

151 Swinburne Row, Newport, RI (401) 846-2722

www.barkingcrab.com

Barking Crab is a rowdy seafood shanty that's been on the (now trendy) Boston Waterfront before it was hip. The beer flows freely and the waterside view makes you feel like you're on the Cape, not minutes from downtown. A breezy open-air tent is packed with picnic tables for family friendly dining during the summer. Indoors is equally fun, filled with buoys, crab traps, lanterns and an island bar. The appetizer menu has it all when it comes to seafood like steamers, fried clams, crab cakes and stuffies. There are several varieties of crab and lobster which can be boiled, bake stuffed or fire grilled. Barking Crab is waterside on Fort Point Channel in South Boston, with an awesome view of the Financial District. There's limited parking in front of the restaurant and huge pay lots adjacent. There's a second location in Newport, RI.

The Cottage

190 Linden St., Wellesley, MA (781) 239-1100

47 Boylston St., Chestnut Hill, MA (617) 916-5413

www.cottagewellesley.com

The Cottage brings the light, fresh cooking of southern California to the suburbs of Boston. The chicken tenders are smothered in a sweet and spicy papaya-Buffalo barbecue sauce with grilled pineapple and blue cheese dip. They're famous for Granola Crusted Mahi Mahi served with brown butter asparagus. Heartier dishes include the mouthwatering half chicken that's marinated with lemon, olive oil, rosemary and sage, then grilled under a brick to make the outside crispy and the inside juicy. The atmosphere is just like the menu: natural and refreshing with hard wood floors, lots of windows and nature scenes on the wall. The kids' menu is one of the best there is, and the service is always quick so the young ones won't get fussy.

Sel de le Terre

774 Boylston St., Boston, MA (617) 266-8800

Natick Mall, 1245 Worcester St., Natick, MA (508) 650-1800

www.seldelaterre.com

Sel de le Terre channels the South of France with oversized decoration, a soaring atrium and a cozy main dining room. Portions are generous, so don't fill up on their famous house-baked bread. This is one of the only "fancy" restaurants that actually encourages parents to bring their kids. The kids' menu is available during lunch, dinner, and brunch with options like pasta, chicken fingers and grilled cheese. The adults will be pleased as well with selections like the ashed ribeye or the pan roasted pork loin. Sel de la Terre is located in the Natick Mall, with plenty of free parking in the garage. At the Boylston location, finding a spot is a bit tougher (and more expensive).

Chunky's Cinema Pub

371 Lowell Ave., Haverhill, MA (978) 374-2200

150 Bridge St., Pelham, NH (603) 635-7499

151 Coliseum Ave., Nashua, NH (603) 880-8055

www.chunkys.com

Chunky's Cinema Pub is one-stop shopping for dinner and a movie. The first-run theater doubles as a full service restaurant. Everyone reclines around long tables in a personal Lincoln Town Car seat where waitresses deliver food and drinks before and during the show. The menu goes way beyond popcorn with appetizers, pub grub and beers by the pitcher. All the menu items are Hollywood themed with Mission Impossible Nachos, Wizard of Ozzarella Sticks and Walk the Line Wings. The Garden State section of the menu offers a variety of salads. Phantom suggests arriving an hour prior to the movie because they do sell out, and it's easier to read the menu before the lights go down.

Noon Hill Grill

530 Main St., Medfield, MA (508) 359-9155

www.noonhillgrill.com

Noon Hill Grill is an upbeat, family friendly restaurant with big booths and a diverse crowd. The new-American menu is equally approachable for sports fans and families. There are juicy, house-smoked wings tossed in apple bourbon barbecue sauce served with celery, carrots and ranch dressing. The marinated steak tips are popular and the barbecue turkey tips fly out of the kitchen. The kids' menu has a much bigger selection than most restaurants with anything from grilled cheese to fish and chips. Desserts are massive and massively delicious, from the strawberry shortcake featuring a fresh-baked biscuit to Sophia's Chocolate Chip Cookies stacked with ice cream, whipped cream and chocolate sauce.

Cheeseboy

www.cheeseboy.com

Cheeseboy is a cute, convenient takeout spot you'll find at malls and transportation centers like South Station serving grilled cheese and hot soups. Customers can choose between four breads, five cheeses, four meats and seven vegetables to make up their favorite version of this nostalgic sandwich. Each one is made to order, so it's always hot, cheesy and grilled until golden brown. There's tomato soup and a selection of the day to dunk your sandwich in. Phantom even visits Cheeseboy for a sweet and orders the Cheeseboy Choco-Melt. Made with Nutella and American cheese on cinnamon swirl bread, it may sound strange, but it's delicious.

French Fries
GREAT ATE

UBurger

140 Tremont St., Boston, MA (857) 239-8080

636 Beacon St., Boston, MA (617) 536-0448

1022 Commonwealth Ave., Boston, MA (617) 487-4855

www.uburgerboston.com

You don't know good fries if you don't know Uburger. This mini fast food chain with three Boston locations stands out for their made from scratch, made to order menu. There are crispy onion rings, creamy shakes, West Coast style griddled burgers and absolutely no heat lamps allowed. UBurger's shoestring fries are hand cut, fried gorgeously golden and portioned generously. Its landmark location in Kenmore Square is a mainstay with students, locals and Red Sox fans alike.

Pier French Fries

12 Old Orchard St., Old Orchard Beach, ME (207) 934-2328

Nothing says summer like sinking your teeth into salty Pier Fries outside in the salt air of Old Orchard Beach. These crinkle-cut creations have been made the same way from this seaside takeout shack for over seventy years. Each golden fry starts with a bag of potatoes that gets dumped into an industrial potato peeler. When all the skin is off, they're hand cut into the famous crinkle configuration. From there, the spuds are cooked once to get the insides soft, then cooked a second time to get the outsides nice and crunchy. There's plenty of ketchup and malt vinegar to douse them, but these fries taste just fine on their own.

Highland Kitchen

150 Highland Ave., Somerville, MA (617) 625-1131

www.highlandkitchen.com

Highland Kitchen is the kind of place you wish you had in your neighborhood. It's totally down to earth with a hopping bar, rocking jukebox and a menu stacked with affordable comfort food. Appetizers include sauteed shrimp and chorizo, Asian marinated steak skewers and Rhode Island style calamari with smoked tomato dipping sauce. For about eleven bucks, there are sandwiches like a

Cuban Rueben layered with roasted pork and corned beef. The terrific Highland Cheeseburger served with perfectly cooked French fries can be ordered on their own for three bucks or doused with chili and cheese for five.

Raising Cane's

949 Commonwealth Ave., Boston, MA (617) 358-5932

www.raisingcanes.com

Located next to BU's Agganis Arena, Raising Cane's is a national fast food chain focused on serving the perfect chicken finger. The menu is short and simple, with only five items. There are chicken fingers, Texas toast, coleslaw, Cane's sauce and crinkle cut fries. These long, ridged fries are soft on the inside and always extra crispy. Their super secret "Cane's Sauce" is spicy, sweet, and savory all at the same time and tastes great on both the chicken and the fries. While honey mustard is not on the menu, Phantom's secret sources tell him it's available if you ask.

The Old Spot

121 Essex St., Salem, MA (978) 745-5656

www.theoldspot.com

The Old Spot in historic Salem is a cozy neighborhood tavern that serves all the comfort food you crave in a space that feels like an old Irish pub. There's the cheesy crock of Four Onion Soup, a massive serving of Fish & Chips and an ultra tasty Reuben. But, the one dish everyone comes for is the outrageously addictive Sweet Potato Sizzler. It's part cheese fries, part nachos and all good topped with English cheddar, bacon, sour cream and scallions over crispy, earthy sweet potato fries.

Halfway Cafe

www.thehalfwaycafe.com

With six locations across Massachusetts, the Halfway Cafe is famous for juicy burgers, crispy pizzas and meaty wings. But it's the hand cut, hall of fame French fries that keep Phantom coming back. These perfectly cooked, skin-on sticks come in a wide variety, from fiery chili to crispy bacon and melted cheese. There are even gravy fries or Buffalo style with a blue cheese crumble. Every Halfway has a comfortable feel with wooden tables and booths, a stocked bar, tons of TVs, free popcorn and scores of framed sports photos on the walls.

JW's Burger Bar

17 New Driftway, Scituate, MA (781) 378-2438

www.jwsburgerbar.com

JW's Burger Bar boasts a yard sale chic vibe that's part Key West cantina, part ski lodge and all incredibly colorful from floor to ceiling. The food is made from scratch, including golden brown fries that are always hand cut in house and served with truffle ketchup. Bodacious burgers are a half-pound of fresh-ground, perfectly seasoned, griddled beef that can be topped with everything from Stilton and caramelized onions to Buffalo sauce and bacon. They even offer a burger shaped cupcake cake for something sweet at the end of your meal.

Five Guys Burgers & Fries

www.fiveguys.com

Five Guys Burgers and Fries is a national counter service chain that's been growing fast for a few years in New England. The dining space isn't much to look at and neither is the menu, serving little more than hamburgers and cheeseburgers with or without bacon. There are fifteen toppings to choose from, all free, so you can load it up without emptying your wallet. No burger is complete without a side of fries. These salty sticks of deliciousness are made from real Idaho potatoes that are hand cut all day long and fried to order so they come out hot, crispy and irresistible. The large is enough to share and typically overflows the container practically filling the entire brown paper bag.

Fried Clams
GREAT ATE

Woodman's of Essex

121 Main St., Essex, MA (978) 768-6057

www.woodmans.com

Woodman's claims to have invented the fried clam way back in 1916. This oversized seafood shack has an upstairs deck and raw bar, a gift shop out back and a scenic picnic area overlooking a serene salt marsh. Quick counter service has customers placing and picking up their orders prior to seating in the casual dining room. Woodman's serves lots of fried seafood, lobster rolls, and perfectly puffy onion rings. However, folks flock to Woodman's for their famed fried clams, encapsulated in a light golden crunch that's adored by natives and tourists who come from all over the world to try this local delicacy.

Beach Plum

17 Ocean Blvd., North Hampton, NH (603) 964-7451

2800 Lafayette Rd., Portsmouth, NH (603) 433-3339

www.lobsterrolls.com

Lined with picnic tables, this no nonsense seafood shack is known for its overstuffed, oversized lobster roll and enormous ice cream sundaes. But it's the fried clams that are truly a plum of a deal. Battered and fried to order, these big bellied bivalves are served with creamy tartar and can be ordered on their own or as part of the Beach Plum's Fisherman's Platter. For a down-home indoor experience, hunker down with your grub on a wooden picnic table at the Portsmouth location. If the weather is nice and you find yourself on the beach, seek out the roadside stand in North Hampton.

Ken's Place

207 Pine Point Rd., Scarborough, ME (207) 883-6611

Ken's is a counter service restaurant that's been serving fresh local seafood since the 1920s including exceptional fried clams. These clams are served two deliciously different ways, either coated with traditional crumbs or fried all puffy in batter. The "crumb" version is lighter and crispier, while the "batter-dipped" recipe is deep fried in a fluffy, donut-like casing. These crispy clams can enjoyed inside their no nonsense dining space or outside on an umbrella lined patio.

Tony's Clam Shop

861 Quincy Shore Dr., Quincy, MA (617) 773-5090

www.tonysclamshop.com

Tony's on Wollaston Beach is an indoor/outdoor, counter service spot adored by generations of seafood fans. Their clams come any style you like: large bellies, small bellies or no belly at all. Some customers love the crispy sweet strips. Others go for the more traditional small bellies. Die-hard clam loving crowds crave the humongous large belly clams that burst with flavor. When Phantom is not clamoring for clams, he sinks his teeth into Tony's famous chicken kabobs or a broiled scallop plate. No day at the beach is complete without some ice cream, and Tony's serves it in cones, frappes and floats. Tony's is seasonal and closed in the winter.

Flo's Clam Shack

4 Wave Ave., Middletown, RI (401) 847-8141

Flo's claims they've served over 20 million of their famous, puffy, crunchy clam cakes since the restaurant opened in 1936. This basic clam shack is decked out in kitschy beach themed décor with a weathered, hand painted sign listing all the usual seafood favorites served on paper plates. Flo ladles out plenty of chowder in both creamy New England and traditional Rhode Island style. The fried clams are light, crispy beauties perfect for snacking after a day at First Beach.

JT Farnham's

88 Eastern Ave., Essex, MA (978) 768-6643

Farnham's sets the fried clam standard high, using only sweet, succulent Ipswich clams. Their rich, soft shells are local delicacies from the nearby, muddy flats. With lots of down-home charm, it's a scenic setting of picnic tables positioned over the Essex Salt Marsh. In the kitchen, the full-bellied critters take a dip in egg wash and corn flour and emerge from the fryolator with a delicate, crunchy coating. That hot, golden garb dissolves instantaneously on the tongue, releasing a scrumptious, savory flavor. They offer beer and wine, but it can only be consumed in the dining room and there's a two drink limit. Bring plenty of cash as they do not accept credit cards.

Red Wing Diner

2235 Providence Hwy., Walpole, MA (508) 668-0453

www.redwingdiner.com

As much as it's known for great food, the Red Wing is also full of history. The front dining room and bar is an authentic Worcester dining car that's maintained the original feel for eight decades. The fried clams are so famous, seaside dwellers make the reverse commute to Walpole for a taste. The kitchen uses plump Ipswich bivalves and a minimal amount of batter, so the true clam taste comes through. For a smaller catch, Phantom loves the broiled scallops, the classic lobster roll and the creamy clam chowder. Red Wing also does one heck of a bar pizza.

Village Restaurant

55 Main St., Essex, MA (978) 768-6400

www.wedigclams.com

At Village Restaurant, the golden Essex clams practically take flight in a light, airy batter and flawless sea flavor. You can trust the clams are super fresh because they're dug locally by clammers whom the owners personally know. Unlike most fried seafood spots, this Cape Ann eatery is a sit-down joint with full service and real silverware. There's lots of local history displayed on the walls in a room that holds a whopping 200 seats. The fresh catches come in generous portions, and the house desserts are divine. There's deep molasses baked Indian pudding, a pumpkin spice pilgrim sundae, and cinnamon Grape-Nut custard.

Fun

GREAT ATE

Ascari Cafe at F1 Boston

290 Wood Rd., Braintree, MA (781) 848-2300

www.f1boston.com

Ladies and gentlemen, rev up your engines! F1 Boston is Phantom's favorite pit stop for a fun night out with a large group or a playful first date. At the area's only indoor go-kart racetrack, you can work up an appetite for pub grub while zipping into a red jumpsuit and racing helmet. Phantom likes to order nachos and burgers at the trackside Ascari Cafe while strategizing on the next go round. They also have a full bar for post race cocktails. A variety of party platters like the "Road America" including Buffalo chicken tenders, potato skins and BBQ wings are perfect for groups of ten. Phantom suggests racing before you eat since a big dinner can weigh you down in the fast lane.

Flatbread Company

45 Day St., Somerville, MA (617) 776-0552

www.flatbreadcompany.com

With locations throughout New England, Flatbread is famous for insanely addictive thin crust pizza cooked in custom built, wood-fired clay ovens. However, it's the Davis Square location that has the perfect balance of food and fun. It's built inside one of the country's original candlepin bowling alleys. No matter where you sit, you see can dough being stretched and pins being smashed. Plus, the restaurant's booths are actually made from old bowling lanes and so is the seventy foot long bar. There are additional locations in Amesbury, Burlington, Martha's Vineyard, Portsmouth and Portland.

Fire + Ice

205 Berkeley St., Boston, MA (617) 482-3473

50 Church St., Cambridge, MA (617) 547-9007

48 Providence Pl., Providence, RI (401) 270-4040

www.fire-ice.com

Fire + Ice is a colorful, quirky, "interactive" dining experience. It's an all-you-can-eat bonanza where customers handpick their meal from a giant spread of seafood, chicken, lamb, turkey, steak, noodles, and forty kinds of veggies. After selecting one of ten sauces like Zesty Pomodoro, Sweet Chili or Fajita, the chefs stir-fry the whole thing at an enormous Mongolian style grill right in the middle of the dining room. Customers are entertained by spatula tricks before they get their sizzling hot grub and stuff it into warm tortillas or pile it on top of fluffy rice.

Howl at the Moon

184 High St., Boston, MA (617) 292-4695

www.howlatthemoon.com

Howl at the Moon in the Financial District features an exciting dueling piano show full of singing, dancing and all around craziness. Two pianists try to outplay each other, as audience members try and outbid each other to get their requests played. Nothing gets the fun flowing like Howl at the Moon's insane eighty-six ounce cocktail buckets. These super sized versions of your favorite mixed drinks are perfect for sharing while the pub style menu is great for snacking. If you're planning a bachelorette party, Howl at the Moon should be on your itinerary for a guaranteed evening of fun.

Tres Gatos

470 Centre St., Jamaica Plain, MA (617) 477-4851

www.tresgatosjp.com

Tres Gatos in Jamaica Plain serves Spanish style tapas and imported meats and cheeses. However, this is no ordinary restaurant. There's a full fledged book and music store in back where a DJ spins all kinds of tunes while hungry diners browse the shelves as they wait for their table. Tasty tapas include a tender Bavette Steak, chorizo spiced Pork Meatballs in a saffron cream and chimichurri sauce or tasty PEI Mussels served in a spicy broth. Funny enough, once the music is flowing, no one ever seems to mind if there's a wait for a table.

Baha Brother's Sandbar Grill

64 Weir St., Taunton, MA (508) 824-2200

www.bahasandbargrill.com

Baha Brother's Sandbar Grill is a little piece of summer all year long. There are surfboards on the walls, fresh seafood on the plates and a Jimmy Buffet-style cover band on stage most nights. The most popular item on the menu is the Big Sexy Burger. It's two 100 percent Angus Beef patties, topped with two slices of melted American cheese and four strips of crispy bacon. Phantom's ultimate Baha Brother's experience always ends with a slice of tangy key lime pie.

Kings

50 Dalton St., Boston, MA (617) 266-2695

600 Legacy Place, Dedham, MA (781) 329-6000

www.kingsbowlamerica.com

Kings takes food and fun to a majestic new level. The atmosphere is outrageous and the numbers are astounding: 26,000 square feet, room for 600 guests, fifty-five High-Def TVs, twenty high-tech bowling alleys, three bars and a 160 seat restaurant that's nothing like the bowling alley food from the past. To start your string off with a strike, order Kings' Sampler Platter overloaded with creamy spinach artichoke dip, fiery Buffalo tenders, bacon blasted potato skins and sesame ginger chicken wings with addictive chili soy sauce. Or, you can roll your way through some Buffalo chicken dip, cheeseburger spring rolls and a crispy chicken salad. From there, the options range from marinated steak tips and baby back ribs to pan-seared scallops and a hand-tossed hamburger pizza studded in special sauce.

Cabby Shack

30 Town Wharf Rd., Plymouth, MA (508) 747-0653

www.cabbyshack.com

The Cabby Shack on historic Plymouth Harbor is the spot for gorgeous views, tons of seats under the sun, live music all summer long and seafood so fresh, it practically jumps straight from the ocean to the kitchen. The Cabby Shack's menu is loaded with fun summer foods like hand battered onion rings, colossal shrimp cocktail, golden fried clams and some of the best bar pizzas on the South Shore. The most famous dish is the ultra-thick and extra-buttery award winning clam chowder, served in a fresh baked bread bowl. Cabby Shack is open year round, so you can have that creamy chowder whenever you want.

Global
GREAT ATE

Blue Ginger

583 Washington St., Wellesley, MA (781) 283-5790

www.ming.com

Blue Ginger is the kind of suburban restaurant for which city dwellers make the reverse commute. Famous for his "East meets West" approach, celebrity chef Ming Tsai can often be seen cooking his signature French influenced Asian cuisine. The spicy Garlic-Black Pepper Lobster retains serious seafood flavor, served beside a lobster shell full of lemongrass fried rice. Mastering Feng Shui atmosphere, the dining room displays Vietnamese waterscapes, rice paper screens, a trickling stone fountain and a forty foot open kitchen. For a more casual experience, visit the lounge for a small plates menu including Ming's Bings: potsticker-like dumplings with a variety of fillings like ginger pork and red roast duck.

Oleana

134 Hampshire St., Cambridge, MA (617) 661-0505

www.oleanarestaurant.com

For Phantom's adventurous palate, Oleana is in a flavor-filled league of its own. The Middle Eastern-influenced menu swirls exotic spice into Mediterranean dishes like sea scallops in tangerine butter. The only difficulty is deciding between fried mussels with hot peppers or za'atar lemon chicken with Turkish pancakes. Not to worry, you can order pre-appetizer bread spreads (Armenian bean and walnut pâté, anyone?) while making up your mind. Equally outrageous desserts include Baked Alaska with passion fruit caramel and chocolate hazelnut baklava. The pretty dining room is intimate and rustic with stone tiling and colorful North African artifacts. There's a gorgeous garden patio in warmer weather.

Moonstones

185 Chelmsford St., Chelmsford, MA (978) 256-7777

www.moonstones110.com

You would never be able to tell that this big, lively restaurant that used to be a Ground Round. Moonstones is taking the sleepy suburbs by storm with a dining room that's sleek and sexy and an international menu full of small plates. It's hard to believe this place is so far outside the city, with sophisticated menu items like seared scallops with lemon oil over truffled potato, rock shrimp tempura tossed in spicy Sriracha, and goat cheese stuffed peppadews with local honey. For customers looking for dishes a little more familiar, there are crispy flatbread pizzas, three styles of wings, hand cut fries with white truffle and Parmesan and even a great bacon cheddar burger.

Towne Stove & Spirits

900 Boylston St., Boston, MA (617) 247-0400

www.towneboston.com

Towne features two floors, three dining rooms, three bars and one of the greatest culinary minds Boston has ever seen, Lydia Shire. Every meal starts with an amazing homemade bread basket, then moves on to dishes from around the world like Kurobuta pork chops and wiener schnitzel. If you're looking for something big, there's Towne's take on clams casino made with one giant sea clam. For over-the-top carnivores, there's the twenty-two ounce Tomahawk Cut Ribeye Steak. There's plenty of lobster on the menu including grilled lobster tails, addictive lobster popovers, creamy lobster bisque and even a wood grilled pizza topped with lobster, corn and honey ricotta.

Addis Red Sea

544 Tremont St., Boston, MA (617) 426-8727

1755 Massachusetts Ave., Cambridge, MA (617) 441-8727

www.addisredsea.com

Addis Red Sea is a transporting Ethiopian experience. Adventurous customers squat on stools and eat with their hands around a tiny woven table. After digging into sambusa tarts filled with beef and lentils, the meal turns to spicy stews and fried meats that are scooped up with thin, spongy flatbread called injera. A grand finale of Harrar coffee is the way to go, since Ethiopia is the motherland of the original bean yielding plant. The dark, smooth brew is deliciously aggressive, infused with cardamom.

AKA Bistro

145 Lincoln Rd., Lincoln, MA (781) 259-9920

www.akabistrolincoln.com

Located twenty miles northwest of Boston, AKA Bistro is a suburban spot so cool, you won't believe it's in Lincoln. This dark, intimate space has an active, open kitchen offering two very distinct menus. One is an authentic French bistro. The other is a cutting-edge Japanese sashimi bar. From the French side of the menu, there's the Moules Frites featuring incredibly crispy hand cut fries and plump mussels in a buttery broth. The Asian menu offers creative cuisine including the addictive rock shrimp tempura tossed in a spicy Korean pepper sauce, an artful arrangement of Hawaiian Amber Jack, or the unforgettable plate of seared tuna and sweet potato tempura.

Street

801 Islington St., Portsmouth, NH (603) 436-0860

www.streetfood360.com

Street may be located in Portsmouth, but the menu reads like a delicious roadmap to the greatest street foods from around the world. This fun, funky spot is set in an industrial, graffiti decorated dining room where customers get to enjoy the kind of foods the natives eat in various countries around the world. Authentic preparations include crispy South American Yucca Fries with Peruvian lime sauce, mouthwatering ribs loaded with Asian flavors, traditional Korean bibimbap and a super stacked Mexican sandwich known as a cemita featuring a slab of fried cheese. The good ol' USA isn't forgotten at Street, because they also happen to make one of the best burgers on the Seacoast.

Diva

246 Elm St., Somerville, MA (617) 629-4963

www.divabistro.com

Diva is a trendy "Indian bistro," set in an upbeat atmosphere with billowing fabric hanging from the ceiling lamps and walls painted in a pleasant olive/yellow with red trim. There's a wide variety of mostly Northern Indian cuisine. The menu is lined with classic currys, vindaloos, and biriyanis that can be ordered mild, medium or hot. Diva's creative menu combines Western influence to Indian classics in dishes like Indian "kulcha tacos", chilli mozzarella naan and even a naan rollup known as the "Naan wich", that can be stuffed with chicken tikka or lamb seekh kebab.

Hot Dogs
GREAT ATE

Spike's Junkyard Dogs

www.spikesjunkyarddogs.com

With several locations throughout Massachusetts and Rhode Island, this local chain with quick counter service delivers all beef hot dogs on oversized French rolls baked in house. The top dog is Spike's original Junkyard Dog topped with sliced tomato, pickles, mustard, scallions and pepperoncini. The Texas Ranger is loaded with barbecue sauce, cheddar and bacon. Phantom's favorite frank would have to be the Buffalo slathered with hot sauce, blue cheese and scallions. Spike's also serves curly fries, Black Angus burgers and chicken sandwiches.

Sullivan's

2080 Day Blvd., Boston, MA (617) 268-5685

www.sullivanscastleisland.com

Set on historic Castle Island in South Boston, Sullivan's is the quintessential all-American hot dog stand. They serve thousands of Kayem old time hot dogs every day, seared perfectly on the grill and placed on buttery toasted buns. For something on the side, Sullivan's onion rings are a must try. They're all hand battered with a thick coat so the crunchy exterior encapsulates every sweet slice. Sullivan's is open from the last weekend in February to the last weekend in November.

Top Dog of Rockport

2 Doyles Cove Rd., Rockport, MA (978) 546-0006

Top Dog is a cozy little hot dog shack with chalkboard walls, a wrap-around counter and hordes of hot dog fanatics. This comfy, rustic, wood lined joint has a menu with more than a dozen creations either grilled or steamed. Diners can then load on toppings like coleslaw, Vidalia onion, carrot relish, bacon, jalapeno peppers and Boston baked beans. If you'd rather not customize your own, Phantom suggests the Golden Retriever Dog covered in indulgent mac and cheese inside a buttered, toasted bun.

Windy City Dogs and More

43 Washington St., Norwell, MA (781) 421-3595

www.windycitydogsandmore.com

A flight to O'Hare is no longer necessary to get your lips on a famous Chicago style hot dog. This classic is served on a soft, poppy seed bun and topped with mustard, onions, tomatoes, a pickle and neon green relish. Windy City offers dozens of dog variations like the Brazilian Dog stacked with mayo, sweet corn and crunchy potato sticks. For a larger appetite, order the Big Scary Manwich featuring two dogs with tamale, chili, cheese and fries on a gut-busting sub roll.

Super Duper Weenie

306 Black Rock Tpke., Fairfield, CT (203) 334-3647

www.superduperweenie.com

A great, convenient snack shack between Boston and New York City, Super Duper Weenie sells split open hot dogs grilled until crispy and plump. All the condiments are made from scratch, including sweet and hot relish, sauerkraut, chili and onion sauce. Their fresh cut shoestring fries are the ideal accessory to a satisfying fast food meal. These long, bronzed twigs are perfectly thin, with a hefty dousing of salt and pepper. Also on the sizzling menu are hamburgers, sausage, cheesesteak and grilled chicken.

George's Coney Island

158 Southbridge St., Worcester, MA (508) 753-4362

www.coneyislandlunch.com

From the sixty foot neon hot dog sign to the graffiti walls carved with customers' names, George's Coney Island is a historic hot dog landmark. The art deco design features wooden booths, tile floors and a stool lined counter. Since 1918, they've been grilling pork and beef wieners served in steamed buns. The links are small and tasty, and the perfect blend of sweet and spicy. The most popular way to order your dog is to get it "up" slathered with mustard, secret recipe chili sauce and chopped onions.

Olneyville N.Y. System

20 Plainfield St., Providence, RI (401) 621-9500

1012 Reservoir Ave., Cranston, RI (401) 275-6031

1744 Mineral Spring Ave., North Providence, RI (401) 383-4155

www.olneyvillenewyorksystem.com

For the ultimate Rhode Island meal, Olneyville New York System is the spot, serving hot wieners, coffee milk and fries "beef stew style". When ordering your dog, ask for it "all the way" with layers of yellow mustard, meat sauce, raw onion, and celery salt on a steamed bun. But, whatever you do, don't call them "hot dogs". New York system refers to the Ocean State's mini links known as hot wieners or "gaggers". The rest of the menu consists of lunch counter staples served to local characters lining the retro booths and long counter.

Flo's Steamed Hot Dogs

1359 Rte. 1, Cape Neddick, ME

www.floshotdogs.com

Since 1959, this legendary, low slung roadside stand has been serving boiled hot dogs topped with Flo's famous house made relish on a squishy steamed bun. Those in the know order a combination of the tangy relish and creamy mayonnaise. The relish is so addictive hot dog fanatics from around the country order it online whenever they want a Flo's fix. If you're looking for a more traditional frank, ask for mustard and a dusting of celery salt. Open year round, the atmosphere at Flo's is basically a small room, a hot dog line, and nothing else. Lines in the summertime look long but move quickly.

Ice Cream
GREAT ATE

Richardson's Ice Cream

156 South Main St., Middleton, MA (978) 7745450

50 Walkers Brook Dr., Reading, MA (781) 944-9121

www.richardsonsicecream.com

Richardson's serves super premium ice cream mixed with milk SO fresh, you can actually meet the cows that make it. This family run operation is located on a dairy farm that dates back over 300 years. They offer classics like banana splits, thick shakes and ice cream sandwiches. With over ninety flavors of ice cream, choosing can be difficult. Phantom's favorite flavor is Moose Tracks featuring a vanilla base with chocolate peanut butter truffles and a fudge swirl throughout. There are batting cages, a driving range and mini golf for post ice cream fun. At their second location in Jordan's Furniture in Reading, you can get your ice cream, hit the IMAX and attend trapeze school, all under one roof.

Gray's Ice Cream

16 East Rd., Tiverton, RI (401) 624-4500

www.graysicecream.com

Gray's is a classic New England roadside ice cream stand that's been whipping up small batches of premium treats for eighty years. Instead of trendy, candy colored flavors, Gray's sticks with the classics like coffee, chocolate chip and butter pecan. Two of the most popular scoops are the Frozen Pudding ice cream and the ginger ice cream made from real ginger root. Since they're open 365 days a year, you can sip on frappes, floats and sodas anytime.

Cedar Hill Dairy Joy

331 North Ave., Weston, MA (781) 894-2600

Dairy Joy is a throwback roadside stand where regulars line up at a blue and white window counter and dine at umbrella covered picnic tables. Fans flock to the Dairy Joy for crispy fried clams and buttery lobster rolls for dinner followed by an icy treat for dessert. The soft serve selections are simply legendary, especially the "Java Berry" swirling creamy coffee ice cream and refreshing raspberry sherbet. Be sure to bring cash as Dairy Joy does not accept credit cards.

Putnam Pantry

255 Newbury St., Danvers, MA (978) 774-2383

www.putnampantry.com

This historic red cottage houses the ultimate ice cream smorgasbord. The all you can top sundae bar is filled with toppings like homemade chocolate sauce, strawberries, crushed Oreos, marshmallow and whipped cream. If you're looking to get into the brain freeze hall of fame, order the monumental monstrosity known as the Battle of Bunker Hill sundae. This mammoth dessert includes seventeen scoops of your favorite flavors. All of this creamy, dreamy goodness can be enjoyed in a quaint, old fashioned dining room that's perfect for birthday parties. If that doesn't satisfy your need for sweets, hit the candy shop on the way out for creamy fudge and nostalgic candies.

Picco

513 Tremont St., Boston, MA (617) 927-0066

www.piccorestaurant.com

Picco in the South End specializes in two of the world's greatest foods: pizza and ice cream. This upscale dining experience doesn't resemble any ice cream stand or pizza shop you've ever seen, with a beautiful outdoor patio and a classy, comfortable dining room. The artisan, hand-crafted pies sport a crispy crust that's almost burnt around the edges. Just like the pizza, Picco's awesome ice creams are made with premium ingredients like Scharffen Berger chocolate, Madagascan vanilla beans and 100 percent Kona coffee. If you want a grown up ice cream beverage, Phantom suggests the "Adult" Ice Cream Soda made with raspberry Belgian Lambic poured over vanilla ice cream.

Ron's Gourmet Ice Cream and 20th Century Bowling

1231 Hyde Park Ave., Hyde Park, MA (617) 364-5274

559 High St., Dedham, MA (781) 326-8664

www.ronsicecream.com

Ron's Gourmet Ice Cream and 20th Century Bowling in Hyde Park is the only place you can get a banana split to go along with your 7-10 split. Bowlers have been known to roll in for the ultra-thick Grape-Nut Frappe, an intoxicating Rum Raisin sundae, and some of the best Black Raspberry on the planet. However, the most sensational scoop is the Caramel Fudge Brownie that's hand mixed with real, fresh baked brownies. While you can't bowl at their Dedham location, you can still get a bowl of your favorite flavor.

Christina's Ice Cream

1255 Cambridge St., Cambridge, MA (617) 492-7021

www.christinasicecream.com

Christina's caters to the adventurous, sophisticated ice cream palate with more than forty insanely inventive flavors inspired by their sister spice shop next door. Basics like Mexican chocolate and garden fresh mint are utterly amazing, but Phantom goes for the exotic cardamom, Japanese adzuki bean, lemon thyme, burnt sugar, white chocolate lavender, saffron and carrot cake flavors. The creamy texture comes from an outstanding fourteen percent butterfat content. The charming décor includes antique church pews and local art. Christina's also concocts exclusive flavors for many of the region's top restaurants.

Kimball Farm

400 Littleton Rd., Westford, MA (978) 486-3891

www.kimballfarm.com

Kimball Farm is an all-American theme park with mini golf, farm animals, a driving range, a country store, bumper boats and phenomenal ice cream. Kids, families and dates flock to this well known and much loved property for a couple of scoops or an entire evening of entertainment. Over forty homemade intriguing flavors like Gingersnap Molasses, Kahlua crunch and Moo Tracks are posted on the barn above a long row of order windows. Kimball's knows that when it comes to ice cream, bigger is better. Cones come in baby, small and large, which are misleading descriptions for the absolutely huge portions. Additional ice cream shops are in Lancaster and Carlisle, MA, plus Jaffrey, NH.

Irish
GREAT ATE

Matt Murphy's

14 Harvard St., Brookline Village, MA (617) 232-0188

www.mattmurphyspub.com

Matt Murphy's is unmistakably Irish with its newspaper-wrapped food, thick accents, and chummy atmosphere. This cozy cubbyhole of a room is crammed with dark wood, crooked wall hangings, a bookshelf of Irish prose, and a stand-up bar. Live music ranging from Celtic to jazz to rock kicks off around 10pm on most nights. The authentic pub serves superior ales and the most memorable Irish fare this side of the pond including complimentary brown bread at every table. Typical Irish plates like Fish and Chips and Shepherd's Pie line the menu. To finish, try the chocolate truffle cake with espresso anglaise and almond praline.

Doyle's

3484 Washington St., Jamaica Plain, MA (617) 524-2345

www.doylescafeboston.com

Doyle's in JP is a rare, old-fashioned pub with old school character. Frequented by political types, the front barroom is packed with wooden booths, red checked tablecloths and a beautiful tin ceiling. The creaky floors and Boston themed murals extend into multiple dining rooms with the same weathered charm. There's plenty of Irish beer on tap (plus fifty others), and the pub grub menu has a great range from pizza to burgers and finger foods. Those in the know go for some clam chowder followed by a Rueben. This is a great stop after taking a tour of the Sam Adams Brewery.

The Tinker's Son

707 Main St., Norwell, MA (781) 561-7361

www.thetinkersson.com

The Tinker's Son takes everything you think about pub food and kicks it up a notch. This dark, wooden, multi-room tavern has the charm of an Irish pub with a lively crowd seated on furniture brought in from the old country. Traditional Shepherd's Pie is served in a cast iron skillet, topped with golden mashed potatoes and gooey melted cheddar. The mac and cheese is baked with a blend of cheddar, Romano, and Swiss. The steak tips are smothered in a rich Guinness barbecue sauce and the ale battered fish and chips are always fresh. On the weekends, a full Irish breakfast complete with Batchelors Beans or a burger topped with an egg over-easy guarantees to cure whatever ails you.

Waxy O'Connor's

94 Hartwell Ave., Lexington, MA (781) 861-9299

121 Main St., Foxboro MA (508) 698-9299

401 Winchester St., Keene, NH (603) 357-9299

www.waxys.com

Waxy O'Connor's serves authentic pub grub in a cozy environment that feels like you're back on the Emerald Isle. Irish fare is the feature, like the Crispy Chicken and Meade or the chunky Guinness Beef Stew, slow cooked for hours so the beef just breaks apart. Even the ribs get an Irish twist, marinated in a combination of Guinness and Magners. For the calorically adventurous, there are traditional Irish bangers, coated in batter and deep-fried. But, if you really want to kill your diet, finish your meal with Waxy's legendary PB&J Bomb: a deep fried peanut butter and jelly sandwich topped with vanilla ice cream.

The Raven's Nest

998 Main St., Walpole, MA (508) 734-9377

www.ravenpubs.com

The Raven's Nest is a family friendly establishment that has an active bar, comfortable dining room and seating outside when it's warm. Flintstonian sized pork chops are cut extra thick and glazed using honey and cinnamon. Tender filet mignon is smothered in a red zinfandel sauce and served with mouthwatering mashed potatoes. Fresh PEI mussels come in a creatively creamy tomato vodka sauce. Along with this upscale fare is the more approachable Bishops Town Burger, topped with Swiss cheese, sautéed onions and mushrooms. Plus, the Raven does brunch on the weekends serving dishes like Grand Marnier French toast or steak tips and eggs.

Lansdowne Pub

9 Lansdowne St., Boston, MA (617) 247-1222

www.lansdownepubboston.com

Lansdowne Pub is an Irish eatery in the shadow of Fenway Park serving outstanding comfort food, live music and plenty of fun. The long wooden bar is perfect for grabbing a pre-game pint. The Lansdowne's menu boats an all-star lineup of authentic Irish dishes kicked up for the American palate like tasty

Irish Sliders with bacon and cheddar or classic hand cut fries smothered in your choice of cheese, gravy or curry. Potato chips are made even more sinful when served alongside a gooey cheese dip. Entrees run the gamut from simple fish and chips to more complex dishes like Fennel Brined Pork Chops smothered in sweet cider sauce. For the ultimate ending to your Irish experience, try the indulgent Guinness Float foaming with creamy ice cream.

Squealing Pig

134 Smith St., Roxbury Crossing, MA (617) 566-6651

www.squealingpigboston.com

The Squealing Pig has everything you want in a pub. There are charming waitresses, over a hundred beers and a fifty foot bar. Tavern treats are turned on their head, like meaty chicken wings coated in an orange chipotle sauce or Tuscan Fries smothered in Parmesan, porcini, and black truffle oil. The pizza is anything but ordinary, topped with everything from grilled shrimp, chorizo and tropical salsa to mashed potatoes, linguica and mustard aioli. The sandwiches (also known as "Toasties") are crispy on the outside and hot and steamy in the center. There are ten varieties, like prosciutto, fig and Gorgonzola or ham, pineapple and pickles. There's even a Mars Bar Toastie featuring a melted candy bar with sliced bananas stuffed between toasted waffles.

Dunn-Gaherin's

344 Elliot St., Newton, MA (617) 527-6271

www.dunngaherins.com

Dunn-Gaherin's is a neighborhood favorite housed in a 170 year old complex that from outside looks more like a Swiss chalet than an Irish pub. Inside, you'll find high beams, exposed brick and memorabilia from Ireland. A welcoming bar greets you at the door with a comfortable dining room in back. Family friendly fare averages well below twenty bucks with appetizers like Buffalo onion rings and fried broccoli bites. The eggplant fries are cooked until crunchy and served with a tangy marinara dip. Comfort food classics include a monster slice of meatloaf and fish and chips with malt vinegar. Dunn-Gaherin's sirloin tips are marinated for hours and include two sides. The place can get packed, but there's complimentary, just popped popcorn while you wait.

Italian
GREAT ATE

Fiorella's

187 North St., Newton, MA (617) 969-9990

www.fiorellasnewton.com

For over ten years, Fiorella's has served consistently great food at surprisingly affordable prices. With a newly expanded bar and dining room featuring an energetic open kitchen, Fiorella's feels like an Italian villa. For starters, every table gets a basket of thin, flat bread sticks topped with oregano, fresh garlic, Romano and Parmesan with a bowl of sweet marinara. They're also known for dishes like softball-sized arancini, Scallops Limoncello, and homemade gnocchi smothered in a plum tomato sauce with dollops of melted mozzarella cheese. Interestingly, the highlight on the dessert menu isn't cannoli or tiramisu. It's the shockingly good apple crisp, baked fresh every day. There are also "express" versions of Fiorella's in Belmont and Brighton.

Da Vinci

162 Columbus Ave., Boston, MA (617) 350-0007

www.davinciboston.com

Da Vinci is a romantic, refined restaurant decked out with fine artwork and eye-catching candelabras with a kitchen that serves modern, Italian cuisine. The unique dining experience starts with a menu that lights up for easy reading in the dimly lit setting. Appetizers run the gamut from fragrant PEI Mussels to a Caprese salad with creamy Burrata cheese. Some of the most popular entrees include the twelve ounce veal chop with porcini mushrooms or the deliciously plump grilled half chicken with white wine and rosemary. The super juicy Da Vinci Beef Tenderloin is Phantom's favorite cut of meat in Boston, made with a red wine demi-glace. The dessert tasting platter features a decadent chocolate soufflé, a crispy baked pear crostata, smooth banana cheesecake, and incredibly creamy house made gelato.

Biagio

123 Moody St., Waltham, MA (781) 891-0100

www.biagiowaltham.com

Biagio offers both Italian and American dishes with global influences. The restaurant is like a giant work of art with gorgeous murals, rustic brick walls, and a winding grand staircase leading up to the ultra-cool lounge. Set on the Charles River, there's an upstairs patio that's perfect for dining on the water when the weather is nice. Starters include an oversized, overloaded antipasto platter, light and crispy calamari and crackly thin-crust pizettas. The entrée side of the menu boasts lobster ravioli in a sherry cream sauce, chicken parm with potato gnocchi, and seared sea scallops with limoncello and white chocolate risotto.

Sweet Basil

942 Great Plain Ave., Needham, MA (781) 444-9600

www.sweetbasilneedham.com

Sweet Basil in Needham is a tiny nook where the wait is always long and the tables are tight. This cash only, BYOB bistro is big on charm with a busy open kitchen in the back. Caesar salad is the real deal, made with a garlicky dressing, Asiago, anchovies and croutons. The pan roasted mozzarella appetizer is served with a tangy basil marinara. Bolognese comes over a hearty portion of handmade papparadelle. Seafood fra diavolo contains the freshest shrimp, mussels, clams, calamari and cod you'll find in a landlocked restaurant. Dessert is not served, and they don't take reservations. Regulars will normally pop into neighboring restaurant bars to have a cocktail while they wait for their table.

L'Andana

86 Cambridge St., Burlington, MA (781) 270-0100

www.landanagrill.com

L'Andana is a swanky Italian restaurant built to look like a Tuscan farmhouse. Decked out in soothing earth tones, weathered planks and chandeliers made from old wine barrels, the cavernous dining room is rustic yet elegant and comfortable. The appealing menu of Tuscan fare varies from house made pastas to enormous steaks and chops grilled to order. The four-cheese fonduta is a great starter to share, served with spicy sopressata, roasted garlic and Tuscan toast. Rigatoni Bolognese comes piled high with al dente pasta and rich, tangy meat sauce. The butter-slathered sirloin is a flawless steak with a dark-charred crust, juicy interior and a deep, smoky flavor from the wood-fired grill. Phantom always orders the piping-hot, molten chocolate cake slathered with sticky salted caramel and honey ice cream to end his meal.

Amelia's Trattoria

111 Harvard St., Cambridge, MA (617) 868-7600

www.ameliastrattoria.com

Amelia's Trattoria in Kendall Square serves rustic Italian food so good, you'd swear someone's grandmother must be in the kitchen. This cozy neighborhood nook has floor to ceiling windows and a highly energetic, partially open, scratch kitchen. Pastas are made on-site every day. The focaccia and fresh garlic bread are baked in house. Meatballs are made with beef, veal and pork topped with melted Fontina and served in a cute mini crockpot. The polenta is a labor of love. It's stirred on the stovetop, then poured out on a board and topped with wild mushrooms, crispy sage, and shaved Parmesan. A tip: The Spaghetti Carbonara featuring pancetta, onions, Parmesan and a sunny side up egg is one of the best dishes, and it's usually not listed on the menu.

Alia

495 Shirley St., Winthrop, MA (617) 539-1600

www.aliaristorante.com

Alia is a quaint BYOB spot with a charming Morroccan chef and incredible Italian cuisine. While every item on Alia's menu is certainly tasty, it's the stuff that's NOT on the menu that has everybody talking. If you call the restaurant within a reasonable time prior to arrival, they'll do their best to prepare anything you like, exactly the way you like it. Dishes that are actually on the menu include slow-cooked lamb osso bucco served in an authentic Moroccan tagine pot. The Ravioli di Nusco is made with sweet Italian sausage and mozzarella that's baked in an intoxicating vodka sauce. Phantom loves ordering Alia's Chicken and Eggplant which is listed as a special but available most nights.

Il Casale

50 Leonard St., Belmont, MA (617) 209-4942

www.ilcasalebelmont.com

Located in a former firehouse, Il Casale's rustic dining room is clad in exposed brick and reclaimed wood. There's a long, lively bar featuring an extensive wine list and a more intimate dining space for a sit down experience. The menu offers century old recipes that have been time tested by chef/owner Dante de Magistris' family throughout the years. Appetizers include a tomato-bread pudding, fried calamari with a crispy lemon wheel and bruschetta with sweet and sour peppers. Pastas like ravioli and gnocchi come in both full and half sizes. For dinner, Phantom recommends the Sicilian roasted chicken prepared in a bright lemon-caper sauce. Family style dinners can be arranged for a flat rate per person.

Lobster
GREAT ATE

Summer Shack

149 Alewife Brook Pkwy., Cambridge, MA (617) 520-9500

www.summershackrestaurant.com

Jasper White's Summer Shack is a big, fun clam shack/restaurant lined with picnic tables for casual dining. James Beard award winning chef Jasper White serves one of Phantom's favorite lobster dishes in the world: the pan-roasted lobster. It's cooked in bourbon and doused in melted butter with chervil and chives. The sweet shellfish is also served wood grilled, baked stuffed with shrimp or wok seared with scallions and ginger. If you're not into lobster, there's down-home fare like corndogs, burgers and Jasper's famous fried chicken. The huge industrial kitchen can feed all 300 seats thanks to a 1,200 gallon lobster tank. There's a smaller Shack in Boston's Back Bay, suburban Shacks in Dedham and Hingham, and a super Shack at Mohegan Sun.

Red's Eats

41 Main St., Wiscasset, ME (207) 882-6128

Since 1977, this seasonal, red and white roadside stand has been home to one of the most famous lobster rolls in the world. Generations of lobster lovers return year after year to patiently wait in line for their turn at the window to feast on one of these incredible sandwiches. Warm drawn butter and cool, creamy mayo are served on the side, so inside the roll is pure, unadulterated lobster meat and nothing else. Red's sells so many lobster rolls, they go through a staggering twenty thousand pounds of lobster meat every season. Since deliveries come in all day long, it doesn't get any fresher.

Chancy Creek Lobster Pier

16 Chauncey Creek Rd., Kittery Point, ME (207) 439-1030

www.chaunceycreek.com

Chauncey Creek Lobster Pier is a rare treasure that combines outdoor dining with clambake cuisine. Crayola colored picnic tables line the deck, and Phantom's favorite seats are along the edge, jutting out over the picturesque water. Chauncey Creek is worth the trek for the fresh air ambiance alone, but the awesome food rounds out the experience. Head to the seafood shack and choose from a New

England menu of live lobsters, fresh crab rolls, steamed mussels in garlic and wine, chowder and peel-and-eat shrimp. Customers can supplement the meal by bringing their own extra sides, wine or beer.

Lobster Pool

329 Granite St., Rockport, MA (978) 546-7808

www.lobsterpoolrestaurant.com

For sixty years, this picturesque dining destination has offered outrageously fresh seafood and amazing sunset views. Lobsters are served simply with French fries and drawn butter. The kitchen cracks the shells, making it easy to satisfy your crustacean craving. Of course, the easiest way to get your hands on some lobster is with a lobster roll. The Lobster Pool's is loaded with chunks of meat and light mayo on a perfectly grilled bun. All this sensational seafood can be enjoyed inside or on outdoor wooden picnic tables overlooking the water.

The Lobster Pot

3155 Cranberry Hwy., East Wareham, MA (508) 759-3876

www.lobsterpotrestaurant.biz

The Lobster Pot on the Buzzards Bay/Wareham line is an eat in the rough, counter service favorite featuring seafood plucked daily straight out of local Cape Cod waters. If you're looking for larger than life lobsters, look no further, because they have them up to ten pounds. They even take special orders for fresh lobsters up to twenty whopping pounds. If you aren't up to all that cracking, you can find huge chunks of tail and claw meat easily, baked into the scrumptious Lazyman's Lobster.

Alive & Kicking Lobsters

269 Putnam Ave., Cambridge, MA (617) 876-0451

www.aliveandkickinglobsters.com

Alive & Kicking Lobsters is a lobster pound and fish market tucked away in Cambridge. It doesn't look like much, and there's really just one reason to go here. A & K makes one of the tastiest sandwiches on the East Coast. Call it amazing. Call it delicious. Just don't call it a Lobster ROLL. This incredible lobster SANDWICH is simply served on toasted, buttered scali bread. Inside is a quarter pound of ultra-fresh shucked lobster meat, a little mayo, salt and pepper. There are no fillers and there's definitely no "roll".

Amrheins

80 West Broadway, South Boston, MA (617) 268-6189

www.amrheinsboston.com

Amrheins in South Boston has been a dining and drinking institution since 1890. No longer just a neighborhood pub, Amrheins has evolved into a truly great restaurant with white tablecloths, a long, gorgeous bar, humongous prime steaks and an all-you-can-eat Sunday brunch. They specialize in upscale comfort food served in a comfortable setting. The ultimate old school favorite that made Amrheins famous is the luscious lobster pie. Chock full of fresh lobster meat and topped with their signature fried lobster claw, this buttery, lemony treat melts in your mouth. There's plenty of free on-site parking.

Arnold's Lobster & Clam Bar

3580 State Hwy., Eastham, MA (508) 255-2575

www.arnoldsrestaurant.com

Along with ultra-crunchy fried clams and baked Wellfleet scallops, this Cape Cod legend has been serving top quality steamed lobsters for over fifty years. Customers come for ice cream, cocktails and a round of mini golf. But, they stay for the three types of lobster rolls. The Regular Roll mixes lobster with a little bit of mayo and fresh squeezed lemon juice. The Hot Roll is packed with just steamed lobster and a side of hot drawn butter. The Ginormous Roll is almost too big for your mouth, with three quarters of a pound of tender, sweet meat. On the side, the Arnold onion rings are a must order. They're hand battered, super skinny and totally irresistible.

Mac & Cheese
GREAT ATE

Mr. Mac's

497 Hooksett Rd., Manhcester, NH (603) 606-1760

www.mr-macs.com

When it comes to macaroni and cheese, nobody does it better than Mr. Mac's. This casual counter service eatery serves mac and cheese customized with a variety of add ons. There are eleven cheeses, fourteen sauces, nine veggies and eleven meats to choose from in small, medium and "The Big Cheese" sizes. There are also house specialties like the Philly Cheese Steak with onions and peppers or the spicy Cajun Mac kicked up with spices and Andouille sausage. There's even a "take and bake" option for a simple solution to tonight's dinner.

Silvertone

69 Bromfield St., Boston, MA (617) 338-7887

www.silvertonedowntown.com

A dark, cool, subterranean mainstay near Downtown Crossing, Silvertone has been a favorite of restaurant industry workers as long as it's been open, which certainly speaks to the food and the affordable yet interesting wine list. Some of Phantom's favorites include the larger than life grilled cheese sandwich and the satisfying Shepherd's Pie. The succulent steak tips have a cult-like following. But, it's the Mac & Cheese that wins the gold on Silvertone's menu. It's topped with buttery breadcrumbs and can be ordered plain or with honey chile chicken, crispy bacon or grilled steak.

The Loft Steak and Chop House

1140 Osgood St., North Andover, MA (978) 686-0026

www.loftsteakandchophouse.com

The Loft is located in the ultimate New England atmosphere, a 160 year old wooden barn with exposed posts and beams. This old school eatery is known for its perfectly cooked steaks, baby back ribs and shrimp scampi. There are four mac and cheese offerings with everything from shaved steak to taco meat. The Phan favorite is the Loft's Famous Lobster Mac & Cheese, loaded with a four cheese blend, spiral pasta and tons of lobster meat throughout. Served piping hot, this is the lobster mac by which all others are judged.

Bar Louie

232 Patriot Place, Foxboro, MA (508) 623-1195

1 Union Station, Providence, RI (401) 427-0600

www.barlouieamerica.com

If you're having a snack attack, Bar Louie is the place to beat it. This dimly lit tavern is lined with flat screens so you can watch the Pats play in Foxboro even if you don't have tickets to the game. Signature items include crispy Buffalo calamari, mini Kobe Beef hot dogs served on a stick and handmade Bavarian pretzels. The menu is lined with burgers and flatbreads. The entrée section includes Sesame Crusted Ahi Tuna, Drunken Fish and Chips, and most importantly, Baked Mac and Cheese. This creamy, dreamy dish is made with a four cheese blend, cooked until perfectly brown on top and can be amped up with add ons like shrimp and fried chicken.

Trina's Starlite Lounge

3 Beacon St., Somerville, MA (617) 576-0006

www.trinastarlitelounge.com

Trina's Starlite Lounge is the kind of neighborhood hangout that concentrates on comfort food served at pocket friendly prices. Standouts include the double Starlite Burger, barbecue sweet potato chips and grilled corn bread. But, if you're really looking for some bang for your buck, dive into the decadent mac and cheese made with oversized shells and big hunks of Ritz Crackers. Regulars suggest a bottle of Miller High Life to wash it all down.

Fox & Hound

123 Sea St., Quincy, MA (617) 471-4030

www.foxandhoundquincy.com

Since 1936, the Fox & Hound has been serving comfort food favorites like the Blue Plate Meatloaf and the Fork & Knife Fried Chicken. There's nothing more comforting than their macaroni and cheese. Each order is made with a heavy helping of Romano, American, goat cheese and extra sharp cheddar. You can also add in roasted tomatoes, chunks of chicken, bacon or lobster meat. This cozy, sophisticated, modern American tavern features a dining room with dark wood tables and a roaring fireplace.

The Publick House

1648 Beacon St., Brookline, MA (617) 277-2880

www.eatgoodfooddrinkbetterbeer.com

The Publick House lives up to its hype as one of the top gastro-pubs in Boston. "Shots: Don't sell 'em", declares the menu. However, you won't care about Cuervo once you've glanced the handpicked beer list with 100 diamond-in-the-rough selections. Their twenty-seven taps are the cleanest in town, serving beer at the proper temperature in the appropriate glassware in a Gothic setting with dueling fireplaces and big screen TVs. All that beer is perfect for washing down some of The Publick House's customizable Baked Mac and Cheese. Diners can add anything from spinach and garlic to bacon, complimenting the perfectly cooked pasta that's enveloped in a five cheese blend.

Grill Next Door

653 Broadway, Haverhill, MA (978) 241-7337

www.thegrillnextdoor.net

Grill Next Door is a triple threat restaurant serving breakfast, lunch and dinner. This come as you are eatery is part diner and part tavern boasting thirty-six brews on draft from all over the world. Lunchtime brings half pound Angus burgers and specialty fries like the Cajun cheese, BBQ chicken or fully loaded with cheddar, bacon, scallions and sour cream. Just as special is the mac and cheese which comes in four styles. You can have it straight up with a buttery cracker crumb crust. The lobster mac is packed with meat. The Buffalo chicken mac bursts with spicy flavor, and the steak bomb mac is loaded with mushrooms, peppers, salami and onions.

Mexican
GREAT ATE

Papagayo

283 Summer St., Boston, MA (617) 423-1000

www.papagayoboston.com

Papagayo is a colorful and stylish cantina that looks more like a tequila museum than a restaurant. Every meal starts with a visit from one of Papagayo's mobile guacamole stations customizing orders for each table. The menu has elevated Mexican dishes like filet mignon fajitas or tasty short rib tacos. Diners can even sink their teeth into a massive Mexican burger or a pan seared shrimp penne tossed in a tequila lime reduction. While the food is certainly delicious, the drinks at Papagayo are the real stars, especially the head-turning, mind-bending Rona Rita: a fruity, frozen margarita topped with an entire bottle of Corona.

La Siesta

70 Woodside Ave., Winthrop, MA (617) 846-2300

www.lasiestarestaurante.com

La Siesta is a warm, family run eatery serving traditional fare fusing authentic ingredients and traditional recipes from owner Martin Vasquez's family. Each meal starts with complimentary salsa and fresh hot chips. The menu features classics like sizzling fajitas with all the fixings. The nightly specials are always spot on, particularly the chicken cutlets served in a poblano cream sauce with spinach and tomatoes. The appetizer menu has wings, queso fundido and twists on classics like crab cakes crusted with tortilla chips. Phantom advises saving room for La Siesta's churros which are served over ice cream and drizzled with chocolate and caramel sauce.

Salsa's

118 Dorchester St., South Boston, MA (617) 269-7878

211 Lincoln St., Hingham, MA (781) 749-9094

www.salsasmexican.com

South Boston and Hingham aren't exactly known for Mexican cuisine. But, a little restaurant named Salsa's is trying to change that. Aptly named for its authentic salsa made with fresh tomatoes, cumin and cilantro, Salsa's has a warm, inviting dining room with funky chandeliers and rich orange walls. No trip is complete without sinking your teeth into their signature Papa Taco, a baked potato stuffed with sour cream, cheese and bacon topped with your choice of grilled chicken or steak. Phantom loves the flavorful Mignon a la Cerveza that's marinated overnight in Mexican beer, garlic and spices.

Mezcal

166 Shrewsbury St., Worcester, MA (508) 926-8307

20 Central St., Leominster, MA (978) 728-4084

www.mezcalcantina.com

Mezcal Tequila Cantina may be the coolest Mexican restaurant north of the Rio Grande. It's an action packed spot with a busy bar that serves margaritas by the pitcher and flights of tequila from an unrivaled list. As for the food, it's all incredibly fresh, colorful and affordable. The guacamole is made to order and served six different ways, like "Tropical" with papaya, mango and roasted cashews. Some house specials include Mexican fish and chips or the pulled pork tostados. The Southwestern Shrimp Scampi is prepared in a tequila butter sauce over rigatoni. The Carne Asada a La Tampiquena is steak topped with pepper and melted jack served with bacon smashed potatoes.

Agave Mexican Bistro

50 State St., Newburyport, MA (978) 499-0428

111 State St., Portsmouth, NH (603) 427-5300

www.agavemexicanbistro.com

Fresh, fun and full of flavor, Agave Mexican Bistro is a lively restaurant where everyone seems to be having a good time all the time. Every meal at Agave starts with fresh homemade corn chips that are cut by hand, fried nice and crisp and brought to the table while they're still warm alongside homemade red and green salsa. Entrees run the gamut from the Seafood Caribe with blackened shrimp and scallops and tender Carne Asada to the gorgeous Chile Relleno stuffed with chicken and cheese. The atmosphere is upscale without being uptight. This three floor space features a cozy bar at ground level, a comfortable dining room on the second floor and a larger, happening bar up top, where a wall of water showcases more than fifty tequilas.

Margaritas

www.margs.com

With fifteen locations throughout Massachusetts and New Hampshire, Margaritas imports artwork and furniture straight from Mexico, and the kitchen turns out your favorite, festive fare. Menu standouts include the crispy chicken chimichangas, sizzling steak fajitas and fresh fish tacos. The fried ice cream boasts a crunchy crushed pretzel coating that's lightly fried and covered in chocolate sauce. While dining at Margaritas, you can't forget to try one of their giant margaritas, frozen or on the rocks. Each is available in a variety of fruit flavors like strawberry basil, raspberry, pomegranate and spiced cider.

Dorado Tacos

401 Harvard St., Brookline, MA (617) 566-2100

www.doradotacos.com

Dorado Tacos is a small, inexpensive counter service taqueria that cooks authentic Mexican fare. Their tacos are the real deal, made with soft homemade tortillas and stuffed with your choice of grilled sirloin steak, marinated chicken, or perfectly charred veggies. The taco Dorado is famous for is the beer battered Ensenada Fish Taco with Baja crema. While the tacos are tops, Dorado also whips up delicious "cemitas". This traditional sandwich hails from Puebla, Mexico and is filled with black beans, chipotle, avocado, Oaxaca cheese and the meat of your choice on a toasted egg roll.

Tu Y Yo

858 Broadway, Somerville, MA (617) 623-5411

66 Chestnut St., Needham, MA (781) 453-1000

www.tuyyo2.com

This humble eatery is clad in old world Mexican photos, painted ceramics and a cobalt –tiled bar. The menu includes family recipes spanning back over a century. Phantom fancies the Chile Relleno, a smoky poblano pepper stuffed with fresh shrimp, goat cheese and black olives and then drizzled with a red bell pepper sauce. The dessert Empanadas are irresistible, filled with dreamy vanilla pudding and coated with thick cinnamon sugar. Tu Y Yo doesn't have a full liquor license, but they do offer ten kinds of Mexican beer and three types of sangria.

Outdoor Dining
GREAT ATE

Casa Romero

30 Gloucester St., Boston, MA (617) 536-4341

www.casaromero.com

Casa Romero is a romantic spot for authentic Mexican cooking. The soft lighting, dark pine wood, and ceramic tiles create a cozy setting inside. The intimate space is hidden down an alley, creating a private dining experience. Outside, there's a charming patio that feels like a secluded secret garden with views of the Prudential Center. Each meal begins with complimentary chips and salsa. From there, diners can choose from traditional fare like the luxurious Pork Tenderloin in a spicy chipotle marinade or the Enchiladas Poblanas stuffed with juicy chicken, melted cheese, sour cream and smothered in mole sauce. With a strong selection of tequilas, Phantom always recommends starting your night with a margarita.

Roof Top Pool at The Colonnade

120 Huntington Ave., Boston, MA (617) 424-7000

www.colonnadehotel.com

Located a dozen stories above Huntington Avenue and miles away from the hustle and bustle below, the Roof Top Pool is like an oasis in a downtown desert. One of Boston's best kept secrets, this one-of-a-kind spot is the city's only roof top bar with a pool open to the public (for around fifty dollars per person). Since most folks are dining in their bathing suits, the menu is geared towards lighter fare with a lineup of sandwiches, salads and small plates. The servers double as life guards, so you won't have to worry about waiting thirty minutes before diving back in the pool after you're done dining.

Gaslight

560 Harrison Ave., Boston, MA (617) 422-0224

www.gaslight560.com

Gaslight is a dark, romantic brasserie creating delectable French comfort foods in a cozy setting. The beautiful, cavernous space is filled with all sorts of authentic touches like subway tiles, burnished mirrors and a sprawling zinc bar. The outdoor patio has high hedges for privacy and heating lamps for when it cools down at night. It's a romantic enclosed space that's set back from the street, so it's very tranquil. During the winter months, you may not want to dine al fresco, but you will want to get your hands on Gaslight's French Onion Soup, draped with a thick layer of hot, melted cheese and packed with sweet onions, salty broth and tender short ribs. Considering the posh neighborhood, prices are reasonable with most entrees below twenty dollars and appetizers in the single digits.

The Farm Bar & Grille

233 Western Ave., Essex, MA (978) 768-0000

www.farmbargrille.com

The Farm is more than just a restaurant. It's an all day experience on an acre of land the owners turned into a massive adult playground. There are always volleyballs being spiked, horseshoes being slung and live music being played over fun fare at pocket friendly prices. With so many outdoor activities, you might think the food would be an afterthought, but nothing could be further from the truth. The Mozzarella Bites are homemade with whole milk mozzarella. The chicken tenders are always fresh, triple dipped, and double fried. The barbecue ribs and chicken are slow smoked the right way. Sister restaurants with similar menus reside in Beverly, MA and Dover and Manchester, NH.

Stephanie's on Newbury

190 Newbury St., Boston, MA (617) 236-0990

www.stephaniesonnewbury.com

The best people watching in Boston probably happens on the patio of Stephanie's on Newbury. This Back Bay mainstay serves everything from comfort food to sophisticated salads with an extensive wine list and top-notch service. While it may be on one of Boston's most prestigious blocks, Stephanie's keeps it casual with classics like meatloaf with caramelized onions or Phantom's favorite bread pudding sweetened with candied apples, caramel and vanilla ice cream. While Stephanie's patio is fantastic, the dining room is a handsome, homey bistro setting with a cozy fireplace and comfortable banquettes.

Eastern Standard

528 Commonwealth Ave., Boston, MA (617) 532-9100

www.easternstandardboston.com

Eastern Standard sets a boisterous, handsome backdrop for upscale bistro dining. A gorgeous, long marble bar enjoys a full view of the spacious room, appointed with rich woods, antique mirrors, and deep red leather banquettes. During warmer weather, their sidewalk seating is some of the city's best outdoor real estate with views of busy Kenmore Square. The menu is mostly country French, but unexpected luxuries, a raw bar, and global dishes catch the diner by mouth-watering surprise. Standouts include flat iron steak, linguine and clams, and day boat haddock. It's great for a pre or post Fenway Park meal, but it can get pretty packed on game days.

Ristorante Fiore

250 Hanover St., Boston, MA (617) 371-1176

www.ristorantefiore.com

Dining in the North End is always special; dining on a North End rooftop is paradise. Fiore is one of the biggest restaurants in Boston's Little Italy, and it's one of the only restaurants in the city with rooftop dining. Take advantage of the full liquor license for a cocktail before ordering an Italian Pinot Grigio to compliment a light and airy pizza. The strength of the menu is in the seafood, like the swordfish with garlic and white wine or the homemade pasta with lobster and shrimp in vodka sauce. After dinner, head across Hanover Street to Modern Pastry for the best cannoli in the neighborhood.

Granary Tavern

170 Milk St., Boston, MA (617) 449-7110

www.granarytavern.com

Located in downtown Boston, just steps from the Greenway, Granary Tavern is equal parts rustic and modern. The building was constructed in 1816 and was originally used as a granary silo. Today, it's completely restored, using original and reclaimed materials, to create the two floor, 250 seat restaurant with a charming sun-soaked patio flanked by large flower boxes. There's a fresh shucked lobster roll packed with knuckle and claw meat and a hint of chive-citrus mayo, served on a griddled brioche roll. The New Orleans style Po' Boy overflows with fried oysters, and the grilled corn on the cob takes a backyard favorite to mouthwatering new heights. Flatbreads range from the traditional margherita to the unique ham and pea.

Pizza
GREAT ATE

Pizzeria Regina

11 ½ Thacher St., Boston, MA (617) 227-0765

www.reginapizzeria.com

Pizzeria Regina is a North End institution covered in neighborhood photos and celebrity guest autographs on the butter colored walls. The cozy, crowded shop is crammed full of warm wooden booths with a tiny bar up front and pizza boxes piled high in every inch of free space. Incredible Neapolitan pizza is the only menu item, made in a piping hot brick oven that's over one hundred years old. A sassy waitstaff serves pies in two sizes: ten or sixteen inches. Both are even better topped with spicy oregano oil, the way real Italians eat pizza. Regina doesn't do dessert, but you can't walk two feet in the North End without tripping over a cannoli. While the original is a must see, you can also get your hands on Regina's pies in malls throughout Massachusetts.

Posto

187 Elm St., Somerville, MA (617) 625-0600

www.pizzeriaposto.com

Posto is a modern rendition of the wood-fired pizzerias you can find in Naples. The centerpiece of the restaurant is a special volcanic rock oven imported from Italy that can withstand temperatures reaching 1,000 degrees. With a temperature so high, each pie cooks in about ninety seconds forming a light, airy crust studded with blackened air bubbles. At most pizza places, a plain cheese pie is pretty plain. At Posto, the Margherita Pizza is the main attraction because of mouth-watering strips of house made mozzarella. For a pie packed with flavor, try the "Porchetta" topped with slow roasted pork, roasted garlic and San Marzano tomatoes or the "Fig" with Gorgonzola cream, applewood bacon and caramelized onions.

Santarpio's

111 Chelsea St., Boston, MA (617) 567-9871

71 Newbury St., Peabody, MA (978) 535-1811

www.santarpiospizza.com

Santarpio's near Logan Airport is a dingy, old school pizza shop with a lengthy bar separated from the dining area. This place has character, with autographed boxing pictures and posters hanging from thin wooden walls, ripped vinyl benches around Formica tables and a jukebox blaring Elvis from the back. The barebones menu lists a couple of barbeque items and simple pizzas with traditional toppings. The perfectly charred pies come in one size, measuring twelve inches. The dough is topped with cheese before a sweet tomato sauce is spread on top. Service can be gruff but that's part of the experience. On the weekend, try to arrive early as a line typically forms out the door during the dinner rush. The newer Peabody location has most of the taste of the original location with less grit.

Cape Cod Cafe

979 Main St., Brockton, MA (508) 583-9420

220 Winter St., Bridgewater, MA (508) 697-3077

995 Broadway, Raynham, MA (508) 802-6599

www.capecodcafepizza.com

Since 1939, the Cape Cod Cafe has been making the South Shore's favorite style of pizza, the bar pie. This crunchy disk of deliciousness is thin-crusted and slightly larger than personal-sized, leaving plenty of room for bar beverages. The atmosphere is old school, the prices are ultra-affordable and the pizza is as good as it's always been, served with all your favorite toppings. Phantom prefers his pizza with "chopped pepperoni" and burnt edges. Alongside the pizzas, the flaky, gooey spinach pie is a must try, and so is one of the Cape Cod Cafe's enormous Greek salads, each one made to order, topped with fluffy feta and homemade dressing.

When Pigs Fly Pizzeria

460 US Rte. 1, Kittery, ME (207) 439-3114

www.sendbread.com

When Pigs Fly Pizzeria is possibly the coolest, most creative pizza place in New England. Inside this modern, industrial space full of wood furniture and metal fixtures, the folks behind the famous When Pigs Fly Breads serve signature crispy pizzas. Hawaiian pizza is given an upgrade when it's made with grilled pineapple and capicola and the Steak & Cheese Bomb pizza is a flavor explosion with peppers, mushrooms and onions. Beyond pizzas, When Pigs Fly Pizzeria has plenty of other options like lobster mac and cheese, tender beef pot roast and hot honey glazed chicken wings. Diners should make sure they order the Cookie Sandwich Trio for dessert. Three fresh baked cookies are filled generously with artisan gelatos and then sauced with gourmet chocolate fudge.

Wicked

660 Legacy Place, Dedham, MA (781) 326-9100

36 South St., Mashpee, MA (508) 477-7422

www.wickedrestaurant.com

Wicked Restaurant is part stylish wine bar, part pizzeria, and part upscale eatery with a menu full of underpriced meals and over the top indulgence. Known for their famous fire-kissed pizza, Wicked thinks outside the box when it comes to toppings. The Scallop BLT pizza tastes like a buttery, crispy version of scallops wrapped in bacon. Meat eaters will fall wicked hard for the pie topped with steak and caramelized onions. The Cape Cod Lobster Bake is a New England inspired pizza loaded with plenty of tail and claw meat, corn and smoked chorizo. If pizza is not your thing, Wicked offers a laundry list of entrees that range from Italian specialties like ravioli and meatballs to creative salads and burgers. For dessert, order the Wicked Mini Donuts, fried to order and served with crème anglais and Belgian chocolate dips.

Pizza Barn

1860 Rte. 16, Center Ossipee, NH (603) 539-2234

www.pizzabarnnh.com

The pies at the Pizza Barn are worth the two hour drive from Boston. For thirty-five years, this real converted barn lined with picnic tables has housed a family friendly pizza parlor that serves the ultimate pepperoni pie. Layered with sweet tomato sauce and lots of oregano, the pizzas are piled with a mountain of thick, hand cut slices of pepperoni that are slightly burnt on the edges. If just pepperoni isn't enough, get your hands on the "Farmer's Daughter" pizza. Coming in between eight and ten pounds, this extra large pie is piled with hamburg, pepperoni, mushrooms, onions and green peppers. Beer can be purchased by the pitcher to share along with your pizza. It's open seven days in the summer; Friday to Sunday only in the winter.

Pino's Pizza

1920-A Beacon St., Brighton, MA (617) 566-6468

www.pinospizza.com

Pino's Pizza has been a Cleveland Circle mainstay and a takeout favorite of

Boston College students on a budget since 1962. A buzzing kitchen provides quick counter service to a small dining room. The traditional Italian pies sport a light, perfectly browned crust. The Sicilian pizza is thick and satisfying with a craveable crust. For under three bucks, you can sink your teeth into a great slice of pepperoni. This hole in the wall also spins specialty pies like the Napoli topped with grilled chicken, broccoli and garlic. The dough is also used to wrap customizable calzones which you can fill with any pizza toppings you wish.

Romantic
GREAT ATE

Cuchi Cuchi

795 Main St., Cambridge, MA (617) 864-2929

www.cuchicuchi.cc

Cuchi Cuchi seduces guests in a flirtatious setting of gypsy lamps, intimate tables and a steamy bar scene where a bordello-chic atmosphere stays classy, amplified by Victorian flair. The fun, commitment-free menu brings international recipes into tapas-style plates like Sizzling Garlic Shrimp and Grilled Skirt Steak with a flavorful chimichurri sauce. The extensive cocktail menu is highly creative with dozens of muddled options. Great for groups with a reservation, but better for a twosome at the bar, this sultry Spanish eatery scores well on all fronts from décor to drinks, dining to dessert.

Lala Rokh

97 Mount Vernon St., Boston, MA (617) 720-5511

www.lalarokh.com

LaLa Rokh on Beacon Hill is a warm, inviting sequence of rooms painted in squash tones and decorated with ancient Persian art, photos, sketches and maps. The homey atmosphere includes fresh flowers, paned glass doors and low-key music. The small six person bar at the entrance is great for diners waiting for a table. The menu is filled with slow cooked, marinated meats like lamb, beef, veal, chicken and fish, often accompanied by chutneys. Dishes embody shocking combinations that work smashingly well, balancing hot and cold. Phantom finds this underrated, authentic restaurant fairly priced for the neighborhood.

White Barn Inn

37 Beach Ave., Kennebunk Beach, ME (207) 967-2321

www.whitebarninn.com

The dazzling White Barn Inn is the ultimate in rustic fine dining, blending collectible antiques and candle lighting with white tablecloths and crystal. The 19th Century barn setting is captivating with decorated lofts, live piano music, and enchanting views through the picture windows. The menu pilots guests through a four course prix fixe menu of designer New England cuisine. Phantom's go to dish is the steamed Maine lobster on a bed of homemade fettuccine with carrot, ginger, snow peas and Cognac coral butter sauce. With formal hospitality from top to bottom, this experience is most certainly worth every penny, especially for very special occasions.

Sorellina

1 Huntington Ave., Boston, MA (617) 412-4600

www.sorellinaboston.com

Sorellina sets a new standard for luxury dining in Boston. The soaring urban space is strikingly modern in black and white with backlit murals, columns, and an entire wall racked with wine. Elaborate pillows line the banquettes, and the gleaming white bar is as eye catching as the suspended glass lanterns. The Italian menu features dressed-up, extravagant fare and homemade pasta. Portions are substantial, which you wouldn't expect for such fancy food like hand cut, sushi grade tuna in a spicy mostarda aioli or the bone-in veal chop with local heirloom tomatoes and Parmesan cheese.

My Place by the Sea

68 Bearskin Neck, Rockport, MA (978) 546-9667

www.myplacebythesea.com

My Place by the Sea is a three-tiered hideaway on the cliffs of Bearskin Neck. Every evening is like a vacation with seating right on the rocks where you can hear the ocean. The outdoor patio sits waterside and is lined with umbrella covered tables with elegant white tablecloths. The kitchen works tirelessly to ensure the food is as memorable as the scenery. The lobster club sandwich is like a kicked up lobster roll served on a freshly baked French baguette. For purists, the classic lobster dinner comes with a side of drawn butter. For meat lovers, My Place has a grilled rack of lamb chops and grilled garlic rubbed sirloin with a sweet yet salty Asian sauce. My Place is seasonal and outdoor seating is weather dependent, so reservations are recommended.

Tangerino

73-83 Main St., Charlestown, MA (617) 242-6009

www.tangierino.com

Tangierino is a lavish date place for a flavorful, authentic North African meal. You'll forget you're in Charlestown as you enter the ornate dining room with tapestry-lined walls featuring red draperies used to create an aura of mystery around the tiled tables and low couches. The sweet-savory creations and couscous tagines will amaze you even more than the live belly dancers. Tagine dishes are a feast for the stomach and the eyes, presented in a cone-shaped clay dish that gently cooks the contents. The Sultan's Kadra perches za'atar spiced, tender lamb atop a tower of cheesy eggplant fritters and rich rosemary reduction. Parking in Charlestown can be difficult, so Phantom recommends springing for valet service.

Chiara

569 High St., Westwood, MA (781) 461-8118

www.chiarabistro.com

Chiara is so handsome, with warm woods and square lamps, you might think you're in Pottery Barn. But, the modern exhibition kitchen under glowing spotlights is a reminder that you're there to eat. Fine touches include an elegant waiting area, a fireplace, and an alcove bar. The bistro menu is classy and well rounded. It changes every six weeks, so you can count on fresh seasonal fare. Portions are big and beautiful with many plates including a small salad and some yummy starch. This is a fine dining establishment, so prices are slightly high for the suburbs, but worth every delicious cent.

Tresca

233 Hanover St., Boston, MA (617) 742-8240

www.trescanorthend.com

Tresca has a menu boasting the latest regional Italian cuisine and a list of hard to find wines. Painted with earth tones, the space sports a handsome wine bar and a wrought iron staircase. Partially owned by Boston Bruins legend Ray Borque, Tresca has the atmosphere of an elegant Italian home with dim lighting and a view of Hanover Street. The regional Italian menu offers a high-end tour of the Boot and includes an entire pasta section, plus a four course tasting. Portions are good from start to finish and pastas can be ordered in smaller sizes if you want to add an extra course like a true Italian. The intimate second floor patio offers one of the most romantic tables in the country: a single two-top hovering directly above Hanover Street.

Sandwich
GREAT ATE

All Star Sandwich Bar

1245 Cambridge St., Cambridge, MA, (617) 868-3065

www.allstarsandwichbar.com

All your sandwich favorites from the Cubano to the Muffalatta to even something as simple as a BLT are at All Star Sandwich Bar. The Atomic Meatloaf Meltdown is a best seller, fired up with Inner Beauty Hot Sauce. The Gobbler goes holiday gourmet with roast turkey, apple sausage stuffing and orange cranberry relish, while the Reuben stacks corned beef on grilled dark rye with Swiss, sauerkraut and Russian dressing. The Beef on Weck piles warm roast beef on a crusty kimmelweck bun, served with horseradish for spreading and au jus for dipping. All Star is a fun, colorful, full-service sandwich bar with cramped seating and a fantastic selection of beer. If pizza is what you're craving, visit their sister restaurant All Star Pizza Bar right across the street.

Sam La Grassa's

44 Province St., Boston, MA (617) 357-6861

www.samlagrassas.com

This weekday lunch only deli boasts "fresh from the pot" corned beef, honey baked ham and aged Black Angus roast beef, all roasted, baked and sliced in-house. Phantom recommends the Famous Rumanian Pastrami Sandwich piled with sweet, ever-so-tender meat. Grilled sandwiches are glorious with combos like the turkey, ham, melted Swiss and creamy coleslaw. Suits and students either grab and go or cram into elbow-to-elbow tables. The cafeteria-style line moves quickly and it's quite a sight to watch the monster meat slicer going nonstop. Sandwiches are about ten bucks, but they're so big and packed with meat, it's actually a great value.

Domenic's

987 Main St., Waltham, MA (781) 899-3817

www.getdoms.com

For more than thirty years, customers have lined out the door for a taste of Domenic's incredible Italian sandwiches with bread made on-site every day. The kitchen makes hundreds of ciabatta rolls by hand and each one comes out of the oven crusty on the outside and impossibly light and chewy on the inside. Every sandwich is made using the best possible ingredients, like the Parma with black label prosciutto, basil marinated tomatoes and fresh mozzarella. Phantom loves the Manzo packed with tender house made garlic roast beef, caramelized onions, gorgonzola and a little bit of arugula. While it's mostly a takeout spot, they also serve everything you'd want in a full Italian meal, like oversized arancini and hand-rolled potato gnocchi.

Parish Cafe

361 Boylston St., Boston, MA (617) 247-4777

493 Massachusetts Ave., Boston, MA (617) 391-0501

www.parishcafe.com

At the Parish Cafe, sandwiches are named after the city's hottest chefs. All the recipes are submitted by the stars themselves, so it's possible to eat their top-notch cuisine at a fraction of the price they'd charge at their own restaurants. The most popular is the Zuni Roll with turkey, bacon and dill Havarti cheese rolled in a crisp flour tortilla. The "Summer Shack" created by Chef Jasper White, puts sea salt and beer battered haddock on a big fluffy roll with lettuce, tomato and remoulade. Ming Tsai created the appropriately named "Blue Ginger": a rare piece of tuna with a teriyaki glaze. The space is artsy with sidewalk seating and a snaking bar serving more than sixty beers.

Nick Varano's Famous Deli

66 Cross St., Boston, MA (617) 391-0050

www.nicksfamousdeli.com

With its prime location at the gateway to the North End, Nick Varano's Famous Deli has quickly become THE spot for overstuffed sandwiches and serious celebrity sightings. The walls are covered with pictures of stars Nick has met over the years, and the menu is packed with sandwiches named after many of those same stars. There's Dom Deluise's Chicken Cutlet with roasted peppers or a rare roast beef sandwich named for boxing legend Rocky Marciano. For diners pretending to eat right, there's the salad "For People Who Don't Really Want a Salad". This gut buster is loaded with "very little iceberg", cucumbers, roast beef, chicken cutlets, mozzarella, onion, bacon, egg and walnuts, served with creamy Italian dressing.

Carl's Steak Subs

55 Prospect St., Waltham, MA (781) 893-9313

www.thecheesesteakguys.com

Forget about Philly; the best cheese steaks in the country come from Carl's, where there's barely enough room for the takeout counter. Their steak bombs pack in over a pound of meat made from a secret two beef blend. There are thirty variations on the original and many have never before been on the steak and cheese circuit. The Firecracker adds in pepperoni and tomato sauce, while the Kamikaze includes sausage, ham, bacon and barbecue sauce. There's also the Misteak with meatballs and sausage, and the Mexican spiced with hot jalapenos. If you can't make it to Carl's, you can score the same steak bombs at their sister restaurants: T.C. Lando's in Acton, Leominster, Clinton and Hudson.

Bob's Italian Food Store

324 Main St., Medford, MA (781) 395-0400

www.bobsfood.com

Bob's is part sandwich shop, part deli and part specialty store. For seventy years and three generations, it's been the place for incredible Italian eats served big, fast and cheap. They make outrageously affordable, oversized platters of stuffed shells, meatballs, and sausage cacciatore. Every sandwich is served on a fresh baked braided roll that's practically exploding with meat. There's gooey steak and cheese, marinated steak tips, a Caprese with prosciutto, and velvety chicken parm. Best of all, these absolutely enormous jumbo-sized subs, packed with a pound of meat, cost about six bucks. If you're looking to feed a few more, there's a giant six foot Italian stuffed with eight pounds of meat, cheese and toppings.

Martino's Liquors & NY Deli

202 Newbury St., Peabody, MA (978) 717-5656

www.martinosliquors.com

New to Route One, Martino's Liquors & NY Deli is a mouthwatering mash up of food and booze. This upscale liquor store is also home to an authentic New York deli, right in the middle of all the wine racks and six packs. Takeout is popular, but there are about a dozen seats to enjoy your sandwich on-site. The Thanksgiving sandwich is made with house roasted turkey breast carved right off the bone and smothered in hot home-style gravy, mounds of stuffing, and cranberry sauce. The French Dip features roast beef topped with caramelized onion and Swiss, served with au jus. The corned beef and pastrami are as good as any New York style deli. They also serve authentic Italian espresso and gourmet coffee drinks.

Seafood
GREAT ATE

Joe Fish

1120 Osgood St., North Andover, MA (978) 685-3663

www.joefish.net

Hot off the grill, steaming out of the sauté pan or served straight from the raw bar, seafood doesn't get any fresher or funkier than at Joe Fish. Check out the Woonsocket Calamari sautéed in garlic butter with cherry peppers. The Haddock Maria is perfectly seasoned and served with mushrooms and artichoke hearts. The massive Fisherman's Feast, anchored by golden fried clams, shrimp, scallops and hand battered onion rings will feed the whole boat. Much like the food, the atmosphere at Joe Fish is colorful and creative with an action packed open kitchen, a busy bar and a cool rain wall with flowing water.

B&G Oysters

550 Tremont St., Boston, MA (617) 423-0550

www.bandgoysters.com

B&G is a designer seafood bar with raised seats lining the marble counters that wrap around the sunken exhibition kitchen. Celebrity chef Barbara Lynch has created a menu lined with dishes ranging from fried fish to more sophisticated selections like sea urchin deviled eggs and pan roasted blue cod with couscous. There are at least a dozen varieties of oysters and cherrystones that are constantly changing. If raw isn't your thing, try the fried Ipswich clams served with tangy house made tartar or the lemony lobster roll packed with tail meat, just enough mayo and a sprinkle of scallions on a buttery toasted bun.

Blue-Eyed Crab

170 Water St., Plymouth, MA (508) 747-6776

www.blue-eyedcrab.com

Take one part New England seafood, add a little Caribbean influence and a few tropical drinks, and you have the Blue-Eyed Crab in Plymouth. This bright, colorful eatery has everything you're looking for in a summertime restaurant anytime of year. Start with the two tiered, twenty item seafood platter, a perfect plate for sharing. The "Crab 2 Ways" features a Panko crusted crab cake over a smooth, creamy crab fondue. True fish fanatics go for the Seafood Stew, which is packed with mussels and chorizo. There's also plenty of fare for meat lovers like the Grilled Pineapple-Rum Marinated Steak Tips or the Grilled Brandy Glazed 30-Day Aged N.Y. Sirloin.

Oceanaire Seafood Room

40 Court St., Boston, MA (617) 742-2277

www.theoceanaire.com

Just steps from City Hall, the Oceanaire feels more like a cruise ship than a restaurant with soaring ceilings, soothing blue lights and an oyster shaped raw bar. With white table cloths gleaming from the dining room, this looks more like a steak house than a place that serves seafood. Since the folks at the Oceanaire want the freshest fish possible, the menu changes daily with dozens of delicious options. However, you can always order golden, full belly fried clams, jumbo-lump crab cakes, or the Oceanaire Surf and Turf, which includes a six ounce filet and a steamed lobster.

Surf

99 Bow St., Portsmouth, NH (603) 334-9855

207 Main St., Nashua, NH (603) 595-9293

www.surfseafood.com

Surf in Nashua and Portsmouth is to seafood what world-class steak houses are to beef. They serve imaginative plates of the freshest fish in a bustling, lively environment. Whether you start with their tower of succulent seafood featuring fresher than fresh oysters, or go for the crab cakes packed with fresh shucked Jonah crab, your taste buds are going to be wowed. If you want some cow with your crustacean, upgrade to the Surf and Turf. This dynamic duo will have you seeing double with a generous portion of filet and crab.

Island Creek Oyster Bar

500 Commonwealth Ave., Boston, MA (617) 532-5300

www.islandcreekoysterbar.com

Island Creek Oyster Bar in Kenmore Square is a sexy place to see and be seen. You know the oysters are the best because Island Creeks are legendary worldwide, raised at their own oyster farm in Duxbury. But, this eatery is more than just a raw bar with fried oyster sliders, local clam chowder and a killer burger topped with maple bacon and Grafton cheddar. Whether you order specials like the Baked Stuffed Lobster or the classic lobster roll, you know the food will be incredibly fresh because chef/owner Jeremy Sewell's cousin just happens to be a lobsterman out of Maine and brings the restaurant nothing but the best.

Fresh Catch

30 Chauncy St., Mansfield, MA (508) 339-5187

24 North St., Medfield, MA (508) 359-6565

473 East Washington St., North Attleboro, MA (508) 695-7087

285 Washington St., North Easton, MA (508) 238-6600

www.freshcatchinc.com

If you love lobster, you'd be crazy not to run as fast as you can to the Fresh Catch. Located adjacent to a seafood market, they serve lobster in several deliciously diverse ways: steamed lobster, baked stuffed lobster, lobster roll, lobster bisque and lobster tails. The best deal on the menu is the absolutely ridiculous Lobster Lover's Delight. It's a six-pound lobster, steamed to perfection and served with a vat of drawn butter. The fish goes way beyond your classic New England standards, with a complete sushi menu as well.

Dry Dock Cafe

7 Drydock Ave., Boston, MA (617) 951-2999

Dry Dock Cafe dishes out gigantic portions of ultra-fresh seafood at ridiculously low prices. Appetizers are big enough to be entrees and include light and airy onion rings, addictive Buffalo scallops and humongous crab cakes bursting with sweet meat. Entrees like The Fisherman's Platter are big in size but not in price. While every restaurant claims to have the freshest seafood, here it's actually true because they're in the same building as North Coast Seafoods, one the country's leading seafood companies. So, while North Coast ships seafood all over the world, the fish at the Dry Dock only has to travel a few feet. The dining room is bright with floor to ceiling windows. While the space itself is informal, there are nice touches like white table cloths. There's free parking, which is rare in Boston. Call ahead as they aren't open every night.

Special Occasion
GREAT ATE

Menton
354 Congress St., Boston, MA (617) 737-0099

www.mentonboston.com

Menton sets the bar when it comes to fine dining in Boston. Named for a French village on the border of Italy, the menu reflects influences from both countries. With a luxuriously simplistic décor, it's easy to see that the focus is on the food. The offerings change frequently as world renowned chef Barbara Lynch likes to work with what's in season. Menton offers guests the choice of two experiences: a four-course prix fixe menu and a more elaborate seven-course chef's tasting with optional wine pairings selected by an acclaimed sommelier. Meters exist on the street, but if you're dining at Menton, chances are you'd valet anyway. Such fine cuisine and service does come at a price. Dinner for two will exceed well over two hundred bucks.

L'Espalier
774 Boylston St., Boston, MA (617) 262-3023

www.lespalier.com

L'Espalier has been a fine dining destination for over thirty years, having moved from its original town house location into the beautiful Mandarin Oriental Hotel. The experience may be sensory overload with stunning views of the Back Bay to jaw-dropping, artful presentations of seafood and meat. The constantly changing menu features dishes like the Maine lobster poached in rich butter for a taste that's absolutely decadent. A fresh heirloom tomato salad with cucumber and white balsamic is a light starter. James Beard award winning chef/owner Frank McClelland also offers prix fixe options with varying amounts of courses included. For the ultimate experience, reserve the Chef's Table and dine inside the L'Espalier kitchen.

Mistral
223 Columbus Ave., Boston, MA (617) 867-9300

www.mistralbistro.com

Mistral has been one of the city's hottest restaurants for a decade with a farmhouse-chic atmosphere of terra cotta floors, mini cypress trees and exposed patches of stone. The dramatic, deafening space accentuates its cathedral ceiling height with stretching columns, glowing luminaries and massive windows. The Mediterranean menu boasts portions that are adequate and elegant, with attention to preparation rather than fanfare. Amazingly executed appetizers include steamed black mussels and their famous tuna tartare with crispy wontons. The entrees are equally impressive with dishes like the grilled tenderloin of Bordelaise style beef or the roast rack of Colorado lamb. While fine dining usually doesn't include grilled pizza, Mistral's rendition is topped with beef tenderloin, mashed potatoes and white truffle oil. Mistral is on Columbus Ave. in the South End, with valet parking boosted by a complimentary car service within two miles of the restaurant.

Hamersley's Bistro

553 Tremont St., Boston, MA (617) 423-2700

www.hamersleysbistro.com

Hamersley's Bistro is a homey, French eatery serving the most exquisite slow roasted chicken. It's utterly juicy, surrendering garlic, lemon and parsley with every single bite. Chef Gordon Hamersley can usually be seen sporting his signature Red Sox cap from the open kitchen, where European cuisine comes together in astoundingly delicious dishes. For starters, try the crispy duck confit with couscous and fig salad. For an entrée, you can't go wrong with the seared sea scallops and lemony endives with pistachios. Pale brick walls, wrought iron candelabras and wooden ceiling beams reinforce the refined country setting.

Arrows Restaurant

41 Berwick Rd., Ogunquit, ME (207) 361-1100

www.arrowsrestaurant.com

When there's a fifty dollar per person cancellation fee, you know you're either being taken for a ride or you're in for something special. Set amidst dense woods and gorgeous gardens, this 18th century farmhouse is highly romantic. Dressed-up diners duck into the wood and glass encased porch, where a sprawling birch tree and square lanterns illuminate a woodland scene. The playful tasting menu and interactive "Chef Collections" change daily, with ninety percent of the restaurant's produce grown on the grounds. They cure their own hams and fish, and each entrée is comprised of multiple tastes and preparations. Seasonal inspirations might include red wine and honey poached beef or cedar plank salmon with rosemary rhubarb candy. Arrows is seasonal, so be sure to call ahead before making your trip North.

Castle Hill Inn

590 Ocean Ave., Newport, RI (401) 849-3800

www.castlehillinn.com

Castle Hill Inn is located in a lovely Victorian mansion with outstanding ocean views. All four dining rooms have a stately, conservative aura from rich, polished woods, thick fabrics and an entourage of servers. For lunch, a must try is the Surf 'N Turf Burger topped with Maine lobster. The dinner menu is much more formal with prix fixe, tasting and degustation menus. Each can be upgraded with wine pairings for an additional fee. The menu is ever changing as the chefs rely on local fisherman and private growers to stock the kitchen.

Bonta

287 Exeter Rd., Hampton, NH (603) 929-7972

www.bonta.net

Bonta is a beautiful, elegant restaurant with high ceilings, a high-class bar and highly delicious Modern Italian cuisine. There's crispy eggplant Parmesan with fresh mozzarella and balsamic roasted tomato sauce and mussels with white wine and grilled ciabatta bread. The slow braised short ribs are served over sweet carrot puree and Gorgonzola creamed spinach. At the bar, Bonta offers half portions of hand cut pastas and a variety of upscale snacks from crispy house made potato chips to the juicy lamb lollipops. Whether you're in the dining room or the bar, you should order the Budino for dessert. This Italian-style pudding is served with a brownie on the bottom that's finished with white chocolate Godiva mousse and a little bit of Heath Bar crunch.

Craigie on Main

853 Main St., Cambridge, MA (617) 497-5511

www.craigieonmain.com

Craigie on Main is an upscale eatery with a casual dining room and four coveted seats at the open kitchen. Chef/owner Tony Maws is so meticulous when it comes to seasonality, every menu lists the time of day it was printed so diners know every ingredient is fresh. There are offerings like the All Natural Sirloin Steak à la Poêle or Vermont Pork Three Ways: suckling confit, spice crusted rib, and smoked and grilled belly. The menu even offers entrees to share like a whole roasted chicken for two with apricots, chanterelle mushrooms and carrots in a Scotch whisky jus. This is one of the only "fine dining" restaurants where you can feel comfortable wearing jeans, and the burger (only available at the bar) is one of the best in Greater Boston.

Sports Bars
GREAT ATE

Game On!

82 Lansdowne St., Boston, MA (617) 351-7001

www.gameonboston.com

Located at the top of Lansdowne Street next to Fenway Park, Game On! is an entertainment destination combining the best in sports viewing and casual American dining. On the first floor, you'll find a bright, colorful bar alongside a bustling dining room. Downstairs, the action is just as packed with tons of flat screens and a view inside the real Fenway batting cage that can be rented for parties. The fare is casual with all your sports bar standards like pizzas, burgers, and truly excellent Buffalo wings. Phantom loves bellying up at the bar in the fall for some Patriots and a Monster Grilled Cheese with creamy tomato soup.

Coolidge Corner Clubhouse

307A Harvard St., Brookline, MA (617) 566-4948

www.thecoolidgecornerclubhouse.com

Affectionately known as the "CCC" to neighborhood sports fans, the Coolidge Corner Clubhouse is a fun place to watch a game and sip some suds. Athlete-named dishes like the Cam Neely burger come with an absurdly giant side of curly fries. Every day, there's a sports trivia question on the menu board, and anyone who answers correctly (no cell phones or internet access allowed!) gets a free slice of chocolate mud pie. A casual brunch is offered on Saturday and Sunday.

Jake n Joe's Sports Grille

475 Providence Hwy., Norwood, MA (781) 349-4880

www.jakenjoes.com

Jake n Joe's is the kind of sports bar you'd expect to see outside Fenway Park or the Garden, but it's right on Route One in Norwood. This sprawling, spacious restaurant caters to fans and families alike with loads of sandwiches, salads and apps. Beyond the flat screen TVs and state of the art beer towers you can tap at your table, Jake n Joe's offers a menu full of finger foods and samplers capable of beating any sized snack attack. The perfect item to share while watching your favorite team is a "JNJ Tower" layered with finger favorites like Buffalo wings, calamari, mozzarella sticks, and Peking ravioli.

Stadium Sports Bar & Grill

232 Old Colony Ave., Boston, MA (617) 269-5100
1495 Hancock St., Quincy, MA (617) 328-0076
342 Moody St., Waltham (781) 609-2445
www.stadiumbars.com

At Stadium Sports Bar, football fanatics are practically at the game with an unobstructed view thanks to thirty flat screen TVs. A prominent bar cuts the handsome wood space down the middle, with plenty of standing room, booths and sports memorabilia. The bar food menu reads like a playbook of good and greasy snacks, sandwiches, salads and classy entrees. The "Nothing But Net" plate is packed with beer battered seafood. Phantom always gets the Bring the Heat burger with Jack cheese, Cajun seasoning, sauteed onion, peppers and crispy jalapenos. The Super Bowl sized portions are served at super prices, insuring you'll have plenty of cash for one of the many draught beers.

Jerry Remy's

1265 Boylston St., Boston, MA (617) 236-7369
250 Northern Ave., Boston, MA (617) 856-7369
www.jerryremys.com

With two prime locations, this sports bar always sports a full house. Since this is former Red Sox player and current announcer Jerry Remy's restaurant, the menu reads like an All-Star team of top prospects. The shockingly big Rem Dawg is a hot dog smothered with spicy chili and melted cheese. The heart-stopping Remy Burger is sandwiched between two slices of golden, delicious fried dough. The Green Monster is an oversized sampler including six hand-formed sliders, eighteen Buffalo wings, a stack of bacon cheesy fries and a cluster of colossal onion rings. In truth, you get a better view of the game at Remy's than you do in the bleachers, with two high-definition projection screens that measure six feet tall and eleven feet wide.

The Fours

166 Canal St., Boston, MA (617) 720-4455

285 Washington St., Norwell, MA (781) 659-4414

15 Cottage Ave., Quincy, MA (617) 471-4447

www.thefours.com

Just opposite the Garden, the Fours was one of the nation's first sports bars, decked out in antique memorabilia, authentic jerseys and autographed pictures. The dark wood dining area surrounds a horseshoe bar with TVs on every side and sports statues guarding the taps. The standard pub grub menu reads like a tasty playbook, naming dishes after famous players and listing categories like "From the Green" (salads) and "Extra Innings" (dessert). Phantom favors the Bobby Orr Steak and Cheese Sandwich: tender, charbroiled steak tips and creamy cheese packed into a sturdy sesame seed roll.

Vito's Tavern

54 Salem St., Boston, MA (857) 277-0229

www.vitostavern.com

With its prime North End location, Vito's Tavern is a great place to watch a game on one of many flat screens or visit before a game at the Garden. In a neighborhood of red sauce Italian joints, this sports bar certainly stands out with quesadillas, burgers and burritos. The wings at Vito's are ultra-addictive, with flavors like chipotle, atomic and Korean style wings served with sweet and tangy sauce. For a sharable twist on the traditional chicken parm dinner, you must try the Chicken Parm Fingers. In addition sports bar staples, Vito's also boasts a line of tacos including Baja steak, Korean pork and fried fish.

Stats Bar & Grille

77 Dorchester St., South Boston, MA (617) 268-9300

www.stats.com

Stats is a ridiculously popular sports bar and eatery with so many flat screens overhead it looks like a TV newsroom. A high ceiling, exposed ducts, brick walls and loud, lively music create a modern, urban vibe. The menu of bar food, pizza and New England style fare has portions so generous, appetizers eat like entrees. The jalapeno cheeseburger offers four levels of heat with jalapeno and cherry peppers, Buffalo-spiked cheddar and smoky chipotle sauce. The flavorful House Pizza is topped with pesto, balsamic-glazed onions, prosciutto, tomatoes and fresh mozzarella. Stats' signature ice cream sandwiches are a great finish, made with luscious house made chocolate chip cookies.

Steak
GREAT ATE

Abe & Louie's

793 Boylston St., Boston, MA (617) 536-6300

www.abeandlouies.com

Abe & Louie's serves the best bone-in filet in Boston. It's the specialty of the house, presented in a portobello demi-glace. Phantom recommends topping it off with aged cheddar cheese or Great Hill blue cheese. Their exquisite Prime steaks come from corn-fed Midwestern beef that's been aged four to five weeks. As for seafood, there's the luxurious shellfish tower that's perfect for sharing or the super fresh grilled swordfish chop. The open space has all the character of a refined steak house, but there's also one of the best bar scenes in the Back Bay. The wine list runs deep, and Abe & Louie's shakes a classic martini at the large mahogany bar. In the fair weather, the scene spills out onto an outdoor patio.

Stockholders

1073 Main St., Weymouth, MA (781) 335-3100

www.stockholderssteakhouse.com

Stockholders is a big, bold, 200 seat spot that brings the feel of a big city steak house to the suburbs. They keep the prices low without skimping on quality with dishes like the perfectly cooked Kona rubbed sirloin, the bone-in cowboy ribeye topped with shallot butter, and filet mignon with a red wine demi-glace. Unlike the city steak houses, sides like sweet butternut squash or cheesy Delmonico potatoes are included with your meal. For lobster lovers, there's the overstuffed lobster BLT, lobster mac and cheese, and an insanely affordable two pound baked stuffed lobster. Stockholders' name and style are inspired by Wall Street. The restaurant is decorated with old stock certificates and pictures of infamous financial figures past and present.

The Capital Grille

900 Boylston St., Boston, MA (617) 262-8900
1 Union Station., Providence, RI (401) 521-5600
250 Boylston St., Chestnut Hill, MA (617) 928-1400
10 Wayside Rd., Burlington, MA (781) 505-4130
www.thecapitalgrille.com

The Capital Grille may be a nationwide chain, but you still get personal attention and all the beef selections you could want. They dry age their beef for two weeks in temperature and humidity-controlled meat lockers with incredibly flavorful results. The Kona coffee-crusted Kansas City strip gains complexity from cracked pepper and caramelized onions, and the porcini rubbed Delmonico boasts gorgeous marbling. Everything is over the top, including crème brulee buried in fresh fruit and a 300 bottle wine list. The atmosphere is just as striking with dark wood, red leather banquettes, marbled lamps and gold-framed art crowding every inch of wall. The new Boston location next to the Hynes Convention Center has the biggest "scene", but the suburban locations offer free parking.

Del Frisco's Double Eagle Steakhouse

250 Northern Ave., Boston, MA (617) 951-1368
www.delfriscos.com

Del Frisco's is a cutting-edge, sexy spot with a huge selection of hand cut steaks, fresher than fresh seafood and unbeatable water views. Of all the restaurants on the wildly popular Boston waterfront, this is the place to see and be seen. The must order meat is the plate-tipping thirty-two ounce Wagyu Longbone. For the indecisive, the Surf and Turf is exceptional, featuring an ultra-tender filet and a succulent Australian lobster tail. Every meal should end with Del Frisco's signature seven layer lemon cake, which weighs in at a whopping two pounds. This is a rare Boston restaurant with a Manhattan vibe.

Tango

464 Massachusetts Ave., Arlington, MA (781) 443-9000
www.tangoarlington.com

Brightly decorated with sunshine yellow patches and exposed brick, Tango is a cozy, intimate space with outstanding Argentinean food. The authentic menu favors beef, beef and more beef, with lots of grilled cuts cooked in Latin flavors. Chimichurri sauce is as common in Argentina as ketchup is in the States, and Tango's version is quite tasty and tangy. The thick herb mélange mixes olive oil, vinegar, minced parsley, oregano, onion and garlic. It's a perfectly light pair with the flank steak or the massive mixed grill for two. Phantom rejoiced when Tango finally added a small bar.

Buckley's Great Steaks

438 Daniel Webster Hwy., Merrimack, NH (603) 424-0995

www.buckleysgreatsteaks.com

Buckley's is a lively, popular steak house situated in an historic tavern. The dining room is decorated simply with white tablecloths and tasteful knickknacks. The expansive menu offers an appealing range of straightforward steak house favorites as well as comfort food like meatloaf and shepherd's pie. The quintessential steak house salad, the wedge is overloaded with heaping portions of blue cheese and smoky bacon. The twenty-eight ounce bone-in Cowboy Steak is marinated before it's cooked over a hardwood fire. The dry aged New York sirloin is rich, beefy and beautifully marbled, topped with a decadent knob of herbed butter. With starters in the low teens and quality steaks in the $20-$30 range, you get a lot of beef for your buck.

New England Steak and Seafood

11 Uxbridge Rd., Mendon, MA (508) 473-5079

www.nesteakandseafood.com

New England Steak and Seafood is a sprawling 700 seat restaurant filled with wood beams and antiques. The steaks are always butchered on-site. Regulars will tell you to order the sirloin blackened, but that has nothing to do with Cajun spices. "Blackened" steaks are simply marinated in a top-secret recipe so the outside is extra crispy and the inside is incredibly tender. The King Cut Prime Rib is their specialty, slow roasted, sliced-to-order and smothered in real pan juices. Every meal starts with a basket full of fresh-baked breads including the signature sticky cinnamon buns, fluffy onion rolls and addictively aromatic pumpkin bread. With the feel of a Vermont ski lodge, New England Steak and Seafood is a popular place to hunker down in the winter.

Mooo

15 Beacon St., Boston, MA (617) 670-2515

www.mooorestaurant.com

Sister restaurant to Mistral and Sorellina, Mooo is located inside the luxurious XV Beacon Hotel. This sophisticated steak house offers breakfast, lunch and dinner, seven days a week. Every meal starts with an order of warm, fresh-baked bread, topped with melted butter and sea salt. The Bone-In Delmonico is a whopping forty-four ounces of tender, juicy meat. The Beef Wellington is eight ounces of luxurious filet topped with spinach and mushrooms, wrapped in puff pastry. Sides can be ordered individually or as part of a "flight", including whipped Yukon gold potatoes, creamed spinach, truffled Parmesan fries and native corn succotash. An extensive wine list guarantees perfect pairings with anything you order. This is a romantic, less masculine steak house that's perfect for a date.

Sushi
GREAT ATE

Oishii Sushi Bar

612 Hammond St., Chestnut Hill, MA (617) 277-7888

1166 Washington St., Boston, MA (617) 482-8868

www.oishiiboston.com

The two Oishii restaurants are as different as can be. The Chestnut Hill outlet is a snug sushi bar with ten coveted counter seats where customers watch sushi experts slice and roll. The South End location is a vast space with high ceilings and stylish, minimal décor. Chef/owner Ting San crafts generous portions of tasty, superbly fresh fish. The salmon shimmers, the red clam comes paper thin and the spicy scallop hand rolls are sublime. The lobster tempura maki is crunchy and delicious and toro is served with white truffle and caviar on top. Hot entrees are equally outstanding with udon noodles and stone grilled selections. There's also a sleek, suburban location in Sudbury.

Wasabi

Natick Collection, 1245 Worcester St., Natick, MA (508) 720-0326

South Shore Plaza, 250 Granite St., Braintree, MA (781) 849-8200

www.wasabisushi.com

Fresh, fun and futuristic, Wasabi has busy shoppers feasting with their eyes before their bellies. With tables lined around a snaking conveyor belt, sushi weaves through an open dining room surrounded by stores and shops. So, when you see something you like, you just reach out and grab it. There's the Red Dragon Roll stuffed and wrapped with ultra fresh tuna. The Baja Roll boasts spicy tuna and jalapenos and the Shrimp Tempura Roll always comes super crunchy. In addition to the sushi, there are plenty of hot entrees as well. While all the adult meals are inventive, the kids menu brings the culinary creativity to a whole new level with a bento box packed with peanut butter and jelly maki.

Douzo

131 Dartmouth St., Boston, MA (617) 859-8886

www.douzosushi.com

In a city where many restaurants speak softly, Douzo shouts out loud with an experimental sushi menu and urban decor. The high ceiling, split level dining room is always buzzing with a busy sushi bar, sleek lounge and banquettes in the back. Japanese cuisine gets a modern makeover with crazy sushi your chopsticks have never seen before. Some hand rolls even skip the rice and wrap with cucumber instead of seaweed. Those who are squeamish about raw fish can order their sushi "torched." On the meat side of this menu, Phantom enjoys the incredibly tender beef tataki served with a bright ponzu sauce. To finish, there's nothing like the tempura sundae with green tea ice cream.

Fugakyu

1280 Beacon St., Brookline, MA (617) 734-1268

621 Boston Post Rd., Sudbury, MA (978) 443-1998

www.fugakyu.net

Fugakyu is an efficiently run Japanese restaurant with traditional charm. An oval sushi bar circulates floating boats of freshly cut fish, while the dining room is a maze of hidden tatami rooms and small, intimate tables closed off by sliding rice paper doors. Lively fish tanks show off future dinners and a huge video screen features beautiful Asian scenery. Kimono-dressed servers deliver fabulously fresh sushi and exquisite traditional fare. The Japanese menu is translated into English, listing pages of traditional and nouveaux Japanese cuisine including sushi, noodles, broiled fish, tempura and stir-fries. The Brookline location claims to be the largest Japanese restaurant in New England while the Sudbury spot is much more intimate.

Uni

370 Commonwealth Ave., Boston, MA (617) 536-7200

www.unisashimibar.com

While Uni is technically located inside the lounge of another restaurant (Clio), it certainly stands alone when it comes to exquisite sushi. The fish is amazingly fresh with certain items sourced directly from Tokyo's Tsuji market, world famous for some of the finest fish in the world. Renowned chef Ken Oringer's meticulous construction of food is magnified when done with something as delicate as sushi. This is clear in dishes like the tuna ceviche with coconut, chilies and lemongrass or the Japanese Amberjack with yellow chive vinaigrette, lily bulb and negri. Amateur sushi lovers should forget this place because Uni is for the most adventurous eaters willing to pay for extremely high quality.

Haru

55 Huntington Ave., Boston, MA (617) 536-0770

www.harusushi.com

Haru in the Prudential Center is part of a chain of sushi bars from New York City. This stylish, modern sushi joint has elegant flowers on each table and window tables overlooking Huntington Avenue. The typical menu lists all your standard sushi like spicy tuna and Philadelphia rolls. However, the sushi really shines in the "special rolls" section of the menu with selections like the Kiss of Fire Roll loaded with tuna, jalapenos and wasabi or the Red Hot Mama Roll with crawfish, mango and cilantro. All your favorite Japanese entrees like chicken katsu and grilled salmon teriyaki come with rice and a soup or salad.

O Ya

9 East St., Boston, MA (617) 654-9900

www.oyarestaurantboston.com

O Ya in the Leather District is a top restaurant for impressing colleagues or getting out of the doghouse with your significant other. This nationally acclaimed sushi spot is dimly lit with very few highly sought after seats. Creative options include hamachi with a spicy banana pepper mousse or the playful "Legs and Eggs" with tiny Maine lobster legs served with white sturgeon caviar. Fish isn't the only thing O Ya gets right, with a list of Wagyu beef dishes on the menu. Since you're blowing your kid's college fund on dinner anyway, you may as well spring for valet in this typically busy neighborhood.

Oga's

915 Worcester St., Natick, MA (508) 653-4338

www.ogasnatick.com

Oga's is very surprising considering it's housed inside a generic looking strip mall. Inside, you'll find Japanese touches like stone, bamboo and a long sushi bar where you can sit right in front of the action. The menu lists almost forty maki rolls and a slew of selections other than sushi like soft shell crab and lobster tempura, shumai and gyoza. There are also some creative flourishes like lamb chop seasoned with thyme, rosemary and black sesame over ginger soy sauce. Master sushi chef Toru Oga is the envy of every knife-slicer in New England for his skill and efficiency with the blade.

Takeout
GREAT ATE

Frigo's

90 William St., Springfield, MA (413) 732-5428

www.frigofoods.com

Frigo's has been perfecting the art of Italian takeout for three generations. It's a neighborhood grocery, butcher shop, bakery and deli all rolled into one. Super fresh cold cuts are stacked and packed on crusty, fresh Vienna rolls. There's the Dirty Italian sandwich packed with fresh-sliced Italian cold cuts and Asiago cheese. The Tanglewood sandwich with roast turkey and dill Havarti cheese is almost too much to finish. Beyond sandwiches, Frigo's also offers full Italian dinners to go, so cooking for the family is almost effortless. There's everything from stuffed pork chops and chicken parm to antipastos and house made sausage with vinegar peppers. In true Italian tradition, they'll let you sample just about anything before you purchase. Frigo's is closed on Sundays.

Blackstrap BBQ

47 Woodside Ave., Winthrop, MA (617) 207-1783

www.blackstrapbbq.com

Blackstrap BBQ is worth the ride to Winthrop Center. With only a few seats inside this bright, funky eatery, takeout seems to be the way to go. The menu is flooded with traditional southern-style plates like meaty ribs and juicy brisket, along with creative sandwiches and decadent sides. The side dish that's so filling it doesn't seem like a side at all is the cayenne crusted mac and cheese that can be amped up with fiery chili for hot heads. Desserts travel well, so if you plan on pigging out, order either the chocolate pecan square or the cornbread pudding with blackstrap rum.

Anna's Taqueria

1412 Beacon St., Brookline, MA (617) 739-7300

www.annastaqueria.com

Anna's Taqueria in Brookline, Boston, Cambridge and Somerville serves perhaps the best burritos in the area. The massive, affordable monsters are made to order with a choice of pulled chicken, grilled steak, veggies or pork. As soon as the tortilla comes out of the steamer, it's a rapid fire race to tell the line cook what you want: beans, rice, salsa, lettuce, guacamole or hot sauce. The whole process takes thirty seconds and it's handed off on a real plate with real silverware. Anna's is perfect for a quick, cheap meal fast, without feeling like you're eating fast food.

Wegmans

9102 Shops Way, Northborough, MA (800) 934-6267

www.wegmans.com

Wegmans is known as the premiere supermarket chain in the country. It's hugely delicious and just plain huge. They specialize in prepared food for eat in or takeout. There are stations set up with sushi rolled on-site, an overloaded salad bar, a smorgasbord of hot Asian food and a bakery churning out fresh breads and pastries. There's a stand that specializes in wings and pizza for the ultimate Sunday afternoon of football watching. Plans are already in the works for new locations in Burlington, Chestnut Hill and Westwood.

Valentino's Kitchen

383 East Dunstable Rd., Nashua, NH (603) 888-7400

www.valentinoskitchen.com

Valentino's is an Italian market with everything you'd expect to find in the North End without the expensive prices you find on Hanover Street. The hand-breaded Chicken Parmigiana is a real "Dish Worth Driving To". For less than eight dollars, you can get a house-roasted turkey club or a Chicken Abbruzzi sub packed with crispy cutlets, thin-sliced prosciutto, fresh mozzarella and balsamic reduction. Valentino's signature "Ring Rolls" can be ordered for any kind of sandwich, featuring a crusty, circular loaf of scali bread big enough to feed the family. Whether you take home some pizza, make yourself a salad, or bring back a fresh-cooked meal to go, you'll want to hit the bakery for some post dinner confections.

Big Daddy's

436 Western Ave., Brighton, MA (617) 787-1080

www.bigdaddyspizza.biz

Big Daddy's is a neighborhood takeout spot that serves all the carbs you love and crave. The space looks like your typical sub shop, but the food is a huge step above. Customers line up for the quick counter service when picking up takeout. There are a few seats for dining on thin, crispy pizza slices pulled right from the oven or calzones filled to the brim with meats and cheeses. Big Daddy's has party sized portions of takeout as well. There's an entire catering menu with platters of pasta, sandwiches and finger foods.

Bailey & Sage

103 State St., Boston, MA (857) 350-3032

www.baileyandsage.com

Bailey & Sage in downtown Boston caters to on-the-go diners that want both taste and convenience. They offer big sandwiches stacked with premium ingredients and hearty chopped salads. Their sandwiches are made with bread hot out of the oven, featuring meats fired on the grill with fresh vegetables. For something slightly lighter, Bailey & Sage also serves salads loaded with so much meat and cheese, even people who don't eat salads will like them. Each one is chopped and sauced to order and served in a unique takeout box that makes it easy to enjoy on the go.

Otto Pizza

1432 Massachusetts Ave., Cambridge, MA (617) 499-3352

289 Harvard St., Brookline, MA (617) 232-0014

888 Commonwealth Ave., Boston, MA (617) 232-0447

www.ottocambridge.com

Originating in Portland, ME, Otto Pizza is an industrial style space with an open kitchen. There are a few salads to compliment the pizza, but the focus is on one thing: hand-tossed pie. Since the menu is so small, they're able to execute creative pizzas perfectly. There's the Pulled Pork and Mango or the Mashed Potato and Bacon. While it may sound crazy, Phantom's favorites are either the Butternut Squash & Cranberry or the over the top Three-Cheese Tortellini Pie. The Cambridge location is tiny and takeout only. In Brookline, you can enjoy a glass of beer or wine at the bar while you wait for your piping hot pie to arrive.

Tapas
GREAT ATE

Bocado

82 Winter St., Worcester, MA (508) 797-1011

www.bocadotapasbar.com

Bocado provides high energy with low lighting, warm colors, provocative pictures and lots of intimate booths. There are over fifty tapas including scallops wrapped in bacon with white truffle honey and fried calamari with garlic, lemon, and orange horseradish cream. For a little bit of everything order the "Bocado Experience". This massive meal includes a charcuterie and cheese plate followed by a sampling of four tapas and a full-sized entrée, like paella stuffed with seasoned rice and your choice of seafood, chicken, or duck confit. This authentic experience ends with traditional desserts like creamy flan or fried churros.

Toro

1704 Washington St., Boston, MA (617) 536-4300

www.toro-restaurant.com

Toro is a dark, crowded, and loud open space with high ceilings, communal tables and a constant buzz. With over fifty items on the menu, there's something for everyone. Regulars in the know typically start out with the Maíz Asado con Alioli y Queso Cotija, a perfectly grilled piece of corn slathered with lime aioli coated in aged cheese. There are meat dishes like the Kabayaki glazed beef short ribs, poultry like the smoked duck drummettes or chicken and potato empanadas with salsa roja, and Catalan stew full of shellfish. The all-Spanish wine list features a variety of bottles including cava that daring diners will sometimes sling back from a traditional porron. Since the food is so good, and they don't take reservations, expect to wait if you go during prime dining hours.

Loco

520 Foundry St., South Easton, MA (508) 230-5626

www.locotapas.com

Loco isn't your typical suburban restaurant. The kitchen specializes in twists on Spanish classics. The dining room sports warm colors and dim lighting while the bar is lively and comfortable. Locals come to Loco for the traditional tapas like the imported Serrano ham or the Sizzling Shrimp sautéed with garlic, olive oil, and herbs. A few of the tapas can make a meal, but if you want to go a more traditional route, Loco offers a range of larger plates like Paella, Stuffed Chicken and Seared Beef Tenderloin with cheese sauce and horseradish mashed potatoes. Phantom likes to end his meal with some creamy Chocolate Flan he's just loco for.

Solea

388 Moody St., Waltham, MA (781) 894-1805

www.solearestaurant.com

Solea is filled with small plates of authentic fare. With colorful lights, flickering candles, funky mirrors and windows that open up to the street, this Moody Street mainstay puts a delicious spin on the flavors of the Mediterranean. There are plates to share like the gooey baked goat cheese, mouth-watering jumbo seared scallops in a pool of saffron cream and the stunning avocado stuffed with crab and mango. Solea's most famous dish is the paella, packed with huge chunks of chorizo, chicken and shellfish cooked in aromatic saffron rice. A cold glass of house made sangria is a refreshing accompaniment to any menu item.

Azorean

133 Washington St., Gloucester, MA (978) 283-5500

www.azoreanrestaurant.com

With an impressive exterior, bustling bar and high ceiling dining room chock full of knickknacks, the Azorean Restaurant is an authentic Portuguese eatery serving large portions of traditional food like paella and shellfish stew. The menu lists thin crust pizzas topped with flavorful chorizo and crispy fried calamari sautéed with olive oil, wine, and vinegar. The tapas menu is made to share, with six plates of deliciousness costing around thirty bucks. Two towers of tasty tapas come to the tables, with choices like smoky grilled linguica or vine-ripe tomatoes stuffed with cheese and baked until bubbly.

Alchemy

3 Duncan St., Gloucester, MA (978) 281-3997

www.alchemybistro.com

Alchemy is a suburban, chic hotspot in the heart of downtown Gloucester. With couches, candles and mismatched furniture, Alchemy offers the comfort of your own living room with a menu of global cuisine. While the menu boasts tapas, Spanish cuisine is just one of their influences. Since you're a stone's throw from the shore, ordering seafood sharing plates like the lobster cake or tuna crudo is an absolute must. Unusual ingredients like squash blossoms are given a Japanese twist when they're tempura fried. Perfectly golden arancini come stuffed with sweet peas and oyster mushrooms over a hazelnut pesto puree.

Kika Tapas

9 Broad Canal Way, Cambridge, MA (617) 245-6030

www.kikatapas.com

Kika Tapas is an ultra funky space clad with eye-popping wallpaper and circular banquettes. The menu boasts both large and small plates. The Paella Valenciana is a perfect entree to share, overflowing with pork sausage, chorizo, chicken and seafood. As for the small plates, Phantom recommends the baby lamb chops cooked with a sweet apricot glaze, melt-in-your-mouth beer braised short ribs, and addictive fried calamari served with a spicy tomato dip. Be sure to wash it all down with one of the dozens of delicious tropical cocktails muddled at the bar.

Tapeo Restaurant and Tapas Bar

266 Newbury St., Boston, MA (617) 267-4799

www.tapeo.com

Tapeo in the Back Bay is a cavernous, two story passport to Spain that's quirky, loud and lively. The festive, dimly lit bar is dripping in dried chili peppers and garlic. Upstairs you'll find copper walls, a fireplace and pretty tiled tables. The menu is mostly hot and cold tapas. There are also interesting entrees like the Zarzuela de Mariscos with shellfish in an aromatic herb and saffron chowder. Phantom loves the Spanish sausage, garlic chicken or shrimp and scallops in saffron cream. Tapeo has a great selection of cavas and rosés that pair beautifully with each dish.

Water View
GREAT ATE

Legal Harborside

270 Northern Ave., Boston, MA (617) 477-2900

www.legalseafoods.com

Legal Harborside is a three tiered, 20,000 square foot palace with waterfront views of Boston Harbor. This multiplex houses three restaurants, a raw bar and a fish market all under one retractable roof. If you've ever been to a Legal Sea Foods, you'll find the fare on the first floor pretty typical with classics like their famous New England clam chowder and Rhode Island stuffies. The second floor is Legal's fine dining experience offering elegant dishes like shrimp cocktail served in an ice shaped sphere. The third floor is a place to see and be seen in the summer with cocktails flowing and a limited menu of sushi and small plates.

Latitude 43 Restaurant & Bar

25 Rogers St., Gloucester, MA (978) 281-0223

www.latfortythree.com

Latitude 43 is absolutely, positively unlike any restaurant you've ever seen. The menu is the perfect combination of surf and turf with seafood options that range from baked stuffed lobster to authentic Japanese sushi. The turf side of the menu includes a skirt steak served with sweet potato "tots" and a juicy rib eye that's infused with bacon and red wine. As delicious as the food may be, it's hard to concentrate on the flavor when the atmosphere is this outrageous with amazing views, an iron sculpted octopus hanging from the ceiling, and a one-of-a-kind sushi pit in the middle of it all.

Sea Ketch

127 Ocean Blvd., Hampton, NH (603) 926-0324

www.seaketch.com

The Sea Ketch on Hampton Beach is a gigantic, seasonal restaurant with four floors of oceanfront dining covering all the bases. There's a bright, sunny dining room with a deck that serves breakfast, lunch, and dinner before it becomes a party under the stars in the evening. The menu has options like the golden, flaky fried fish sandwich, a larger than life lobster roll or the Sea Ketch Surf and Turf, with fresh lobster medallions and tender filet mignon. Breakfast also includes seafood dishes like New England Eggs and Lobster Claws served in a warm hollandaise sauce with homefries. The roof is for the party crowd, with live music and cocktails.

Harborside Grille & Patio at the Hyatt Harborside

101 Harborside Dr., East Boston, MA (617) 568-1234

www.harborside.hyatt.com

Spectacular scenery and the finest local fare come together at the Harborside Grill inside the Hyatt Harborside Hotel at Logan Airport. Inside the dining room or outside on the patio, diners are treated to sprawling views of the harbor and downtown Boston skyline while eating hearty plates of New England comfort food. There are light starters like the grilled flatbread pizza and more hearty dishes like the lobster mac and cheese served alongside an extra lobster tail. For the ultimate ending to your meal, the perfect dessert is the warm cinnamon apple tart with a scoop of vanilla ice cream.

Seaglass Oceanside Restaurant

4 Ocean Front North, Salisbury, MA (978) 462-5800

www.seaglassoceanside.com

Seaglass is a posh seaside restaurant with front-row views of the crashing surf of Salisbury Beach. The soft plinking of piano keys and a refined decor of muted whites, grays, and sandstones create an elegant yet comfortable ambience. Fresh-caught seafood is the star of the menu, but there are dozens of appealing options for carnivores and vegetarians. With entrees prices in the $30s, you'll need to shell out some serious clams, but it's worth the money for entrees like the perfectly cooked bone-in ribeye, golden fried clams or the big, buttery and beautiful baked stuffed lobster.

Red Rock Bistro

141 Humphrey St., Swampscott, MA (781) 595-1414

www.redrockbistro.com

Red Rock Bistro is a waterfront dining dream come true with stunning views of the Atlantic and a creative menu of fare from land and sea. The patio is clad with industrial stainless steel tables and chairs situated right on the water. The leopard printed but cozy dining room is lined with floor to ceiling windows for the ultimate oceanside view. Red Rock offers an ultra-fresh raw bar, creative pizzas topped with lobster, sweet corn, and blue cheese, and entrees like the juicy center cut filet mignon with roasted garlic butter. Be sure to stop in for brunch when they offer Bloody Marys and live jazz music.

Inn at Bay Pointe

64 Washington Ct., Quincy, MA (617) 472-3200

www.innatbaypointe.com

Down a residential side street overlooking the water and just steps from the marina, you'll find the Inn at Bay Pointe (if you're lucky). As beautiful as the setting may be, the folks at Inn at Bay Pointe knew the quirky location meant they needed to wow the crowds with top-quality food at a lower-than expected price. So, they lined the menu with monster portions priced way below what you'd pay downtown. The most popular dish is the overflowing baked stuffed lobster. The tanker-sized prime rib is a mouthwatering mammoth with a fresh-baked popover on the side. With entrees tipping the scale at twenty bucks, this is one of the best deals on the South Shore.

Waterman Grille

4 Richmond Sq., Providence, RI (401) 521-9229

www.watermangrille.com

The Waterman Grille is a cozy eatery with a bustling open kitchen, dark wooden interior and beautiful panoramic views of the Seekonk River. During the season, you may catch the Brown crew team on a practice row. The menu at Waterman is chock full of all the dishes you love, like barbecue short ribs and crispy pizzas. All the meat is perfectly cooked on a wood-burning grill. The filet mignon is juicy and served with a sweet potato gratin, while the Maple Brined Pork Porterhouse is cooked perfectly pink and served with a decadent Talegio bacon bread pudding. The chocolate mousse cake is so dense and fudgy, you may want to share it.

Wings
GREAT ATE

Sparky's Wings and Things

20 Emerson St., Haverhill, MA (978) 521-1009

www.sparkyswings.biz

This neighborhood spot's motto is "Come for the wings. Stay for the things", and since the space is so small, it serves mostly takeout. With twenty flavors of bold, sizeable wings, you may have trouble deciding. The Dragon's Breath has a garlicky goodness. The Wicked PB & J wing might be the most delicious, flavored with Thai peanut and raspberry habanero sauce. All these addictive wings come in sizes that range between five and one hundred. Beyond chicken, Sparky's "things" include plenty of creative burgers, crispy fries and hot dogs topped with chili or cheese.

Kowloon

948 Broadway, Saugus, MA (781) 233-0077

www.kowloonrestaurant.com

It's almost impossible to describe the Kowloon to anyone who has never experienced this Asian food and entertainment complex. Owned and operated by the Wong family since 1950, the Kowloon has evolved into a landmark on Route One in Saugus. With seating for nearly 1,200 customers, it's a mind-bogglingly large operation featuring Chinese food, a Thai kitchen and a sushi bar under one roof. While all the Asian fare is divine, nothing tops the Saugus wings. This sticky-sweet, ultra-garlicky chicken is addictive and pairs perfectly with their signature mai tais or scorpion bowls.

Chicken Bone

358 Waverley St., Framingham, MA (508) 879-1138

www.thechickenbone.com

The Chicken Bone might look like a biker bar from the outside, but they make some of the biggest and best chicken wings you've ever tasted. There's the lip smacking on the bone wings, or a mouthwatering boneless version. "The Bone" offers thirteen sauces including honey barbecue, teriyaki, sticky sesame and thermonuclear. When you're not sucking down those wings, you can soak in some suds over some live music or in front of one of their HD flat screen TVs.

They do tons of takeout and delivery for those who want to enjoy some wings and pizza in the comfort of their own home.

Angela's Coal Fired Pizza

880 Broadway, Saugus, MA (781) 941-2625
361 Middlesex Rd., Tyngsboro, MA (978) 649-8312
www.angelascfp.com

Angela's brings the old fashioned cooking technique of coal firing to the masses in the form of crispy pizzas and flavorful wings. The name on the door of this warm, inviting restaurant may read "Pizza", but it's the famous signature coal fired wings that are the real attraction. Each wing is marinated in lemon juice, olive oil, rosemary and garlic and then roasted in 900 degree coal-fired ovens. They're served piled high on top of homemade focaccia bread and smothered in caramelized onions. You should order one of Angela's gloriously charred pizzas to accompany your wings.

Buff's Pub

317 Washington St., Newton, MA (617) 332-9134
www.buffspubofnewton.com

Buff's Pub is a no-frills, neighborhood watering hole that serves comfort food favorites in a down to earth environment. The large buffalo head mounted on the wall is the first clue that this pub is serious about wings. Made only from farm fresh chicken that's never been frozen, the outstanding finger food would probably take flight if not grounded in heavenly sauce. The traditional BBQ wings are extra thick through the middle and deep fried to render the joints crunchy. Slightly sweeter versions include honey hot and honey BBQ. Other pub grub includes deep-dish potato skins and beef soft tacos. As an all-American watering hole, Buff's is lined with beer ads and bar stools, with plenty of brews on tap.

Eat at Jumbo's

688 Broadway, Somerville, MA (617) 666-5862
www.eatatjumbos.com

There's no beating eating at Eat at Jumbo's in Ball Square. This Somerville takeout mainstay serves oversized subs, piping hot pizzas and all kinds of fries. The wings are tossed to order in loads of flavors spicy and sweet. There are classics like Buffalo and General Gau or more funky, fruity flavors like Raspberry BBQ or Teriyaki Pineapple. Once you've finished your wings, you have got to lay your lips on one of Jumbo's crazy burgers, hand tossed pizzas or Phantom's favorite, the Steazy Cheezy Garlic Sticks.

Harry's Bar & Grille

407 West Grove St., Middleboro, MA (508) 947-9297

www.harrysbarandgrille.com

This loud and lively pub has food everyone loves, at prices anyone can afford. With an airplane theme throughout, it's only natural that the Jumbo Jet Wings are a top seller. Rather than cutting them into two pieces, Harry's keeps them whole. Entrees include grilled steak tips, whole belly fried clams and a magnificently messy burger topped with bacon, cheddar, onion rings and bourbon barbecue sauce. For dessert, Phantom loves the Shaky Bones Sundae: a peanut butter filled Funny Bone snack cake warmed up and topped with premium vanilla ice cream, rich hot fudge and plenty of whipped cream.

PizZing's Pizza & Wings

1840 Ocean St., Marshfield, MA (781) 834-3040

1035 Bedford St., Abington, MA (781) 792-0003

www.pizzingspizza.com

PizZing's is a casual family friendly restaurant specializing in two things: pizza and wings. They offer twenty-five types of stone baked pizzas, and over fifty flavors of chicken wings ranging from six to ninety-six per order. There's a flavor for every one of your taste buds including the sweet and spicy Honey Heat, the Sticky Scotchman and the hothead favorite, the OMG. For folks wanting something on the super sweet side try the Flyin' Hawaiian: an addictive wing soaked in sweet tangy sauce with a pineapple finish. For both pizza and wings together, the eighteen-inch Buffalo Supreme Pizza is definitely different, made with a Chile Lime Buffalo sauce.

PHANTOM GOURMET

GREAT ATES

by Location

Back Bay
GREAT ATE

Clio

370 Commonwealth Ave., Boston, MA (617) 536-7200

www.cliorestaurant.com

Clio's understated elegance and extreme cuisine make for an unpredictably special splurge. Pale walls, a lattice ceiling, and leopard skin carpets create an uptown setting for a downtown clientele. Chef/owner Ken Oringer crafts a wildly artistic menu, where European and Asian influences are shaken up with incredibly rare ingredients and food lab experiments like foams and infusions. The ingenious results are palate-challenging, like lacquered foie gras with sweet and sour lemon and bee pollen. Phantom also loves the salmon tartare with avocado, gold beets, and red ginger. Oringer can often be seen at Uni, the annexed sashimi bar downstairs.

Sonsie

327 Newbury St., Boston, MA (617) 351-2500

www.sonsieboston.com

Sonsie has a scene-seeking crowd packed into marble cafe tables, with frequent celebrity sightings and a front row view of the Newbury Street sidewalk. The dining room is clad with comfortable leather sofas for a relaxing night of eating and drinking. The basement wine bar is less of a scene and makes for a more intimate experience. Lime crab cakes and open face steak sandwiches give way to perfectly executed pastas, brick oven pizzas and entrees like steak au poive. Don't pass on insanely good desserts like baby éclairs and blackberry sorbet with citrus curd. Once dinner is done, Sonsie turns into a chic spot serving elegant cocktails to an upscale crowd, making it the ultimate combination of a bar and restaurant.

Grill 23 & Bar

161 Berkeley St., Boston, MA (617) 542-2255
www.grill23.com

Grill 23 & Bar is a stately space of power dining with massive marble columns, high detailed ceilings and elegant tables positioned so everyone can see everyone. A lineup of chefs work the exhibition kitchen and the old money atmosphere continues upstairs with private wine rooms. Servers wear butcher jackets and even escort guests to the bathroom instead of just pointing. The superior steak house menu presents prime beef and day boat seafood in a la carte and creative entrée options. Plus, there's the added bonus of a raw bar menu.

Lolita Cocina & Tequila Bar

271 Dartmouth St., Boston, MA (617) 369-5609

www.lolitaboston.com

Lolita is like a sexy underground lair where the aphrodisiac of choice is high-end tequila and modern Mexican cuisine. Every meal at Lolita starts with a complimentary Grapefruit and Mint Granita, a Mexican-style slush that's topped with tequila and served over a bubbling cauldron. Believe it or not, there's another eye-popping freebie at the end of dinner: fresh-spun sour apple cotton candy that's sprinkled with cherry Pop Rocks. After dinner most customers make their way to the bar, where the provocative red lights, flickering candles and eye-catching cast iron plays backdrop to hand-crafted cocktails like the spicy cucumber margarita.

Via Matta

79 Park Plaza, Boston, MA (617) 422-0008

www.viamattarestaurant.com

Via Matta is sleek and elegant with mosaic tiles, antique iron and lustrous glass panels that tie together the dining room, wine bar, patio and late night cafe. Star chef Michael Schlow writes a stunning Italian menu representing regions from Piedmont to Tuscany. Portions are perfectly executed and plentiful, but vegetable sides must be ordered separately. The menu is lined with pastas like spaghetti with tiny clams, cherry tomatoes, and parsley, cavatelli with braised rabbit, and tagliatelle alla Bolognese. Elegant entrees like sirloin with fennel, white beans, and shiitake mushrooms are beautifully presented. Visit their enoteca before or after your meal for a glass of wine from the extensive selection.

Atlantic Fish

761 Boylston St., Boston, MA (617) 267-4000

www.atlanticfishco.com

Atlantic Fish is a seafood haven with a steak house-style ambience. Wood paneling, high ceilings and low lighting create a comfortable vibe, while the expansive bar bustles with an after work crowd. The catch of the day is served simply grilled or broiled, or showcased in inventive recipes. The shellfish platter is a towering smorgasbord of fresh crab, oysters, shrimp, lobster, and littleneck clams, served with several tangy dipping sauces. Whole-belly clams are deep fried light and crisp and cooled with creamy tartar sauce. The New England Lobster Feast is festive and includes a two pound steamed lobster served with clam chowder, mussels, steamers, corn on the cob, and new potatoes. The menu at brunch features an outrageous Eggs Benedict, topped with lobster and filet mignon.

Met Back Bay

279 Dartmouth St., Boston, MA (617) 267-0451

www.metbackbay.com

With a selection of rooms for different dining experiences, including an exclusive lounge next door, Met Back Bay is really one restaurant with multiple personalities. There's a sophisticated library bar for sipping on martinis, a formal dining room for a special night out, and a lively basement lounge complete with a ham and cheese bar. They serve breakfast, lunch and dinner Monday through Saturday, with a sophisticated brunch on Sunday. There are plenty of seafood options on the menu, like lobster rolls and swordfish skewers, but steak is where the Met really shines. There's filet, prime skirt steak, New York sirloin and a forty-two day wet aged prime center ribeye served with a variety of house made sauces.

Forum

755 Boylston St., Boston, MA (857) 991-1831

www.forumboston.com

Forum is essentially a duplex of deliciousness. When you walk in, there's a lively dining room to your right that extends into patio seating outside. There's an oval shaped bar packed with thirty something professionals sipping stiff martinis. Upstairs, you'll find a smaller, more intimate bar and a big, bustling room where diners have a bird's eye view of Boylston Street. The menu is upscale but not pretentious with wings, tacos and sliders served as starters. Phantom is a huge Phan of the Lobster Ricotta Gnocchi in a beurre blanc and sorrel pesto sauce or the grilled swordfish with tomato and fennel salad. For a decadent night of dining, begin with some oysters, followed by filet mignon, and end with the flourless chocolate cake

Beacon Hill
GREAT ATE

No. 9 Park

9 Park St., Boston, MA (617) 742-9991

www.no9park.com

No. 9 Park is the ultimate Beacon Hill destination, overlooking the Boston Common from a 19th century mansion. James Beard award winning chef/owner Barbara Lynch's country European cuisine includes masterful creations like roasted lamb chops with preserved lemon. The gnocchi, made from Idaho potatoes, is by far her best dish, dressed in luxurious accents like prunes and seared foie gras, pumpkin, lobster or even truffle oil. For an over-the-top adventure, order the seven course tasting menu paired with rare wines from boutique vintners. The retro-elegant dining area features intimate tables while silk shirted servers work the Italian marble bar tables.

Grotto

37 Bowdoin St., Boston, MA (617) 227-3434

www.grottorestaurant.com

With artsy style, Grotto promises decadent cuisine at outstanding prices. The spunky space is perfect for a romantic meal or a fashionable lunch with your favorite politician. Out of the way and below street level with few seats and no bar, this place survives because of its reputation for great food. The free-form Italian menu is hearty with excellent daily specials. The Caped Critic likes to start by dipping grilled steak tips in a bubbling cheese fondue of rich Fontina and truffle oil. The Fra Diavolo Butter Poached Lobster is served on a bed of linguine with spicy tomato sauce. For the ultimate value, try Grotto's prix fixe meal (offered seven days a week) which includes three courses for less than forty dollars.

Scampo

215 Charles St., Boston, MA (617) 536-2100

www.scampoboston.com

Located inside the Liberty Hotel, Lydia Shire's Scampo is a dimly lit hot spot with great outdoor dining when the weather is right. There's an open kitchen cooking some of the most creative Italian cuisine in Boston. The best way to start any meal at Scampo is an order of freshly baked bread. Rosemary Focaccia is covered with soft Robiola cheese, sprinkled with sea salt, and drizzled with a sweet red wine sauce. The "Elephant Ear Walking" is a warm, cracker-thin treat, painted with tomato sauce, cheese and basil. For a unique experience, guests can pull up a seat at the mozzarella bar and watch as house-made cheese is prepared seven different ways, like on top of thinly-sliced prosciutto or stacked with king crab meat and avocado. Wood-fired pizza also goes gourmet with toppings like lamb or hunks of fresh lobster meat.

The Paramount

44 Charles St., Boston, MA (617) 720-1152

www.paramountboston.com

The Paramount is a neighborhood coffee shop turned yuppie, with cafeteria-style service by day and sit-down, white linen dinners by night. The narrow front room maintains a simple but modern atmosphere with patches of brick wall and elbow-to-elbow diners at silver-lined seats. Further back, there's a sleek open kitchen opposite four high-topped tables. The organized flow at busy breakfasts mandates customers not take their seats until their food is served. Breakfast includes all the A.M. standards like omelettes, pancakes and French toast topped with bananas and caramel. The simple afternoon menu includes standard burgers, fancy salads and griddle sandwiches. Portions are as large and filling as The Paramount is small and cramped. There's a new location in South Boston.

75 Chestnut

75 Chestnut St., Boston, MA (617) 227-2175

www.75chestnut.com

Tucked into a side street, this dimly-lit, brick-clad hideaway is a local favorite known for being casual, comfortable and friendly. As you walk in, you're greeted by a humongous tray of free cheese and crackers. There's a big wooden bar that's perfect for grabbing a post work drink and snack. The menu is focused on New England classics like pork chops and fish and chips. There's everything from a half-pound burger completely covered with melted cheese to an upscale filet mignon with roasted potatoes and crispy onion straws. Phantom loves the Crème Brulee Collection for dessert, featuring three small brulees in various flavors. Sunday brunch offers classic Eggs Benedict and more creative items like Stuffed Lobster Hash and Raspberry Stuffed French Toast.

Bin 26 Enoteca

26 Charles St., Boston, MA (617) 723-5939
www.bin26.com

Bin 26 Enoteca is one big wine party, except that it's closet-size small. Anyone looking to brush up on wine vocab (there's a glossary of terms in the wine list) can do just that while snacking on everything from imported cheese to a full-on Mediterranean meal. Wine is clearly the theme with a corkboard collection, racked bottles, a wall of wine labels and a cool ceiling of suspended bottles in the bathroom. The awesome hanger steak is sliced into intensely flavorful, buttery cuts and cooked in Chianti sauce. For dessert, the "ThreeRamisu" has a trio of fun interpretations of tiramisu: the traditional creamy square, a rich liquid drink, and sweet gelato studded with a cookie. Wine pours come in three sizes so you can experiment or enjoy a full glass.

Tip Tap Room

138 Cambridge St., Boston, MA (857) 350-3344
www.thetiptaproom.com

The Tip Tap Room has a variety of inventive tips and thirty-six tap beers. Every type of tip you'd imagine is on the menu, including house marinated steak with horseradish potatoes, fresh swordfish with an artichoke and bell pepper salsa or lamb soaked in a mint and shallot marinade. For the adventurous, there's a rotation of more exotic meats like antelope, goat, rabbit, emu and yak. There's a loaded appetizer menu with some of the tastiest potato skins Phantom has ever had, filled with bacon, beer cheese sauce and a fried oyster. The space is typically full with enthusiastic patrons making it loud but fun. During the warmer months, the garage door style exterior is lifted, so you almost feel like you're dining al fresco.

Toscano

47 Charles St., Boston, MA (617) 723-4090
www.toscanoboston.com

Toscano has been a neighborhood standby for decades, but a recent renovation gave the dining room a multi-million dollar make-over with exposed brick, a gorgeous marble bar and hand-carved wooden doors. The pasta course is when Toscano's kitchen really shines. There's hearty penne in a rich Tuscan-style meat sauce or the show-stopping "Rigatoni Toscano" studded with double smoked bacon, tomato cream and fresh herbs. The pizzas are impossibly thin and delicious, from the Quattro Formaggio with sliced tomatoes and fresh arugula to homemade sausage and fresh mozzarella. Toscano's 1,000 bottle all-Italian wine list is stored in a state-of-the-art, temperature controlled wine room. Considering the neighborhood, the space and the food, diners will be very surprised at how reasonable the bill is.

Cambridge
GREAT ATE

Area Four

500 Technology Sq., Cambridge, MA (617) 758-4444

www.areafour.com

Area Four is a sleek urban cafe and restaurant with a stylish decor of steel, wood and polished concrete. The double-high ceiling and wall of windows give the dining room a cheery, spacious vibe with plenty of natural light. The menu of shareable plates, featuring local and seasonal ingredients, is a tempting tray of options with portions so small you'll need a few to fill up. Approachable fare lines the menu with tapas like terrific house made mozzarella and entrees like the meatloaf cheeseburger or mac and cheese topped with buttery croissant crumbs. An extensive list of pizza includes one topped with cherrystones and bacon and another topped with pepperoni, sausage, meatball and bacon. Large pizzas range in the low twenties, but each crunchy bite is worth every cent.

Basta Pasta

319 Western Ave., Cambridge, MA (617) 576-6672

www.bastapastacambridge.com

Basta Pasta is a small space with a few tables and counter service. The chalkboard menu is lined with authentic Italian preparations from dressings and sauces to meatballs and desserts. Phantom favorites include the mini arancini stuffed with Fontina cheese or mussels brimming with garlic, lemon and white wine. The mainstay at Basta Pasta is the old-style, wood-fired brick pizza oven. Options range from the classic Margherita pizza sprinkled with fresh chopped basil to grilled chicken with homemade pesto. But, "pasta" is part of the name, so you need to use your noodle and order the pasta Bolognese tossed with homemade fusilli. A second "enoteca" style location is in Quincy.

Cataylst

300 Technology Sq., Cambridge, MA 02139 (617) 576-3000

www.catalystrestaurant.com

Catalyst is a vast space with a tempting menu. The industrial setting is dimly lit with an eye-catching double-sided fireplace. The perfect way to warm up your palette is Catalyst's fiery chicken wings with creamy tzatziki dipping sauce The burger is topped with roasted tomatoes, caramelized onions, cheddar and bacon on a brioche bun to hold it all together. There are also more elegant eats like tournedos of beef topped with Taleggio ravioli and a red wine demi-glace, and the handmade cavatelli in a cherry pepper pesto. The decadent chocolate fondant with a hazelnut streusel and banana coulis is a great ending to your meal.

Chez Henri

1 Shepard St., Cambridge, MA (617) 354-8980

www.chezhenri.com

Chez Henri near Porter Square is a warm, vibrant bistro swept up in rich red colors and vibrant still life paintings. If you're on a date, escape to the intimate barroom where the lights are turned low. The bold menu highlights local fish, dividing attention between Cuban and French dishes. There's also a nightly prix fixe of three courses. Most come for the incredibly popular pressed Cuban sandwiches that can only be ordered at the bar. Seating at the bar is first come first serve, and the bartender has a running tab on "who's next". In the main dining room, you'll find French fare like steak frites and lobster pot au feu served with Cuban classics like red snapper steamed in banana leaf.

East by Northeast

1128 Cambridge St., Cambridge, MA (617) 876-0286

www.exnecambridge.com

East by Northeast in Inman Square is tucked into a tiny storefront with a handful of tables, plus four stools perched at a compact bar. Low-lit and cozy, the intimate space is decked out in Asian woodcarvings, soothing earth tones and chalkboards bearing market-fresh daily specials. Pan-Asian tapas runs the gamut from inventive salads and dumplings to house made noodles. The carb-fest of a menu is nourishing and filling, and you can order extras like five-spice boiled peanuts for a few dollars more. Dessert is not offered, but sugar fiends can hit Christina's Homemade Ice Cream a few blocks away.

Hungry Mother

233 Cardinal Medeiros Ave., Cambridge, MA (617) 499-0090

www.hungrymothercambridge.com

Hungry Mother's space feels like the corner of an old Virginia plantation with white walls, dark wood floors and a soaring ceiling. The appealing menu of Southern comfort grub is short and sweet with nothing but nostalgic favorites like deviled eggs and a gourmet version of grits. Portions are generous and you can always add on terrific Southern snacks like the spicy house made pimiento cheese or salty boiled peanuts. Hungry Mother is steps from the Kendall Square Theater lot which offers inexpensive parking if you can't find a meter. Single digit appetizers and entrees in the low twenties will have you whistling "Dixie."

Lord Hobo

92 Hampshire St., Cambridge, MA (617) 250-8454

www.lordhobo.com

Lord Hobo in East Cambridge is a serious gastropub and chilled-out hangout in the old B-Side Lounge space. Dark red walls, stark light bulbs suspended from a cavernous ceiling and forty plus obscure beers on tap create a brooding, hipster atmosphere. The menu specializes in lager-friendly comfort food like burgers and steak tips, plus more ambitious fare like the seared scallops with cucumber-tomato salad. Portions are on the modest side, leaving enough room for a rich, hoppy brew or two. There are no desserts at Lord Hobo, but you can satisfy your sweet tooth with a glass of double-chocolate stout or finish the meal with a cheese plate. Street parking can be difficult as it's mostly resident-only in this neighborhood.

East Side Bar & Grille

561 Cambridge St., East Cambridge, MA (617) 661-3278

www.eastsidebarandgrille.com

East Side Bar & Grille seems more like a place you'd find in the North End than East Cambridge. The menu is loaded with Italian comfort classics with appetizers big enough for the entire table. There's the extra cheesy eggplant rollatini stuffed with ricotta and Romano or the mountain of mussels sautéed in garlic and oil. A loud, enthusiastic crowd of regulars feast nightly on hearty pasta Bolognese with slow simmered beef and sweet sausage, Shrimp Bianco with garlic and sun dried tomatoes and the larger than life portion of chicken parm. East Side also has plenty of meals from the grill, like burgers, steak tips, shockingly great BBQ ribs and Italian meatloaf made with a special blend of beef and sausage.

Cape Cod
GREAT ATE

Mac's Shack

91 Commercial St., Wellfleet, MA (508) 349-6333

www.macsseafood.com

From the outside, Mac's Shack looks like your typical Cape Cod clam shack. The old white building sits along Duck Creek with a fisherman statue hauling in a giant lobster on the roof. The outdoor bar is always packed with people having a great time over adult cocktails. When it comes to the seafood, they keep it simple and let the fish speak for itself. There are Wellfleet oysters shucked at the outdoor raw bar, sweet and juicy broiled sea scallops and traditional Cape Cod lobster steamed in seawater and served with corn on the cob. There's even a full sushi bar, slicing up stuff so fresh it practically swims to your plate. There's a second clam shack style location right down the street on the Wellfleet town pier.

Baxter's

177 Pleasant St., Hyannis Port, MA (508) 775-4490

www.baxterscapecod.com

Baxter's in Hyannis features two fun waterside eateries in one. The Boathouse Club is a casual full-service area with a lively bar and cloth captains' chairs around nautical map-top tables. Alternatively, Baxter's Fish & Chips is ideal for takeout and counter service with a shack-style atmosphere of wooden booths, fishing rods in the rafters and outdoor picnic tables on a pier. Both sides use the same kitchen and the extensive seafood menu includes coconut shrimp, lobster salad, native steamers and baked stuffed lobster. This is a quintessential Cape experience that will cost less than twenty-five dollars for substantial entrees.

Pain D'Avignon

15 Hinckley Rd., Hyannis, MA (508) 778-8588

www.paindavignon.com

Pan D'Avignon is one of the best bread bakeries in the country, and it's home to a world class restaurant that's most definitely road trip worthy. Down a lonely road near the airport in Hyannis, Pain D'Avignon is massive, 15,000 square foot facility where 185 deliciously different pies, pastries and breads are made by hand every day. The bakery starts the day with flaky croissants for breakfast.

At lunch, they serve slices of stone hearth pizza and outstanding sandwiches like the black forest ham and melted Gruyere on focaccia. At the end of the dinner, dessert brings silky smooth brioche bread pudding, a flavor-packed blueberry pie and a decadent brownie sundae. At night, the full bistro menu features more substantial items like steak frites.

Kream 'N Kone

961 Main St., West Dennis, MA (508) 394-0808

www.kreamnkone.com

Kream 'N Kone is a Cape Cod favorite with legendary fried seafood including some of Phantom's favorite clam strips. Without the messy whole bellies (which some people might not like), all that's left is the neck and perfectly crisp breading. They're wonderfully tender, fried to a gorgeous fourteen karat color with just enough chew. Kream 'N Kone also offers seven kinds of seafood rolls, outstanding onion rings and twenty-four flavors of soft serve. Their newly remodeled, air conditioned space is large and great for groups. There's also outdoor seating right on Swan River.

Roadhouse Cafe

488 South St., Hyannis, MA (508) 775-2386

www.roadhousecafe.com

Inside this inviting yellow building in Hyannis, there's a casual all-American bistro that serves everything Phantom Phans love to eat like fire-grilled steaks, ocean-fresh seafood, pizza, barbecue and stick-to-your-ribs comfort food. The atmosphere at the Roadhouse walks the line between fun and refined, featuring colorful antiques and a classy piano bar. Entrees include a generous portion of Zuppa di Pesce or the Roadside Surf and Turf: a tender eight ounce filet mignon served with an open faced lobster stuffed generously. The Grilled Double Cut Stuffed Pork Chop is massive and loaded with prosciutto, spinach, roasted red peppers and melted mozzarella, finished off with an exquisite port wine demi-glace.

Bleu

10 Market St., Mashpee, MA (508) 539-7907

www.bleurestaurant.com

Bleu in Mashpee is a flirty space that falls somewhere between traditional bistro and hipster hangout. Wing backed chairs line the aqua tiled wine bar, while the dining room transitions from an all-wood alcove of black leather banquettes, vintage posters and marble tabletops to deep underwater walls decorated in antique mirrors and paper lanterns. The menu goes in two distinct directions with bistro French dishes separated from Asian trendy fare. For a sweet way to end your meal, Bleu includes chocolate truffles with the check.

Chillingsworth

2449 Main St., Brewster, MA (508) 896-3640

www.chillingsworth.com

Chillingsworth is set in a charming manor of squat ceilings, period wallpaper and corner hutches. Situated in the 300 year old Chillingsworth Foster estate, this eatery is made for special occasions. The setting presents a country manor-meets-Cape Cod setting for relaxed fine dining. They offer a tasting menu that includes a seven course meal of French cuisine with modern sparkle. For those folks seeking a more casual dining experience, Chillingsworth's sister restaurant, Chills Bistro, offers great cuisine without requiring the time it takes to finish multiple courses.

Captain Kidd

77 Water St., Woods Hole, MA (508) 548-8563

www.thecaptainkidd.com

Captain Kidd offers casual dining right on the water. Whether you belly up to the pirate themed bar, bring the family for some casual dining or have an intimate evening with a special someone at a table on the dock, they've got you covered. The menu has elegant dishes like broiled sea scallops with Panko bread crumbs or pan seared halibut with mango Salsa. For purists, there's more traditional Cape Cod fare like the creamy New England clam chowder or a classic steamed lobster plucked from the waters outside.

350 Grill

350 Worthington St., Springfield, MA (413) 439-0666

www.350grill.net

With its brick walls, oversized banquettes and color changing bar, the 350 Grill is a surprisingly classy restaurant considering it shares a parking lot with a gentlemen's club. Customers love the tapas style appetizers like sushi grade tuna tartare, homestyle veal meatballs served on a sizzling skillet and the eggplant tower stacked with house made mozzarella cheese. On the entree side of the menu, 350 Grill boasts gourmet offerings like the coffee-crusted pork tenderloin topped with bacon in a light Kahlua cream sauce, twin baked lobster tails with lemon butter or the meticulously plated frutti di mare. The surf and turf is a towering, head turner of a dish stacked with two scallops, filet mignon and jumbo shrimp smothered in a luxurious cheese sauce.

Bub's BBQ

676 Amherst Rd., Sunderland, MA (413) 548-9630

www.bubsbbq.com

Less than two hours west of Boston, Bub's BBQ is a roadside shack where people go to pig out. With red and white checkered tablecloths inside and picnic tables outside, Bub's is the kind of place where you can roll up your sleeves and get messy. All of Bub's meats are slow smoked over hickory wood and slathered with addictive homemade sauce. While people come for the barbecue, they keep coming back for the unlimited sides. There's a buffet loaded with fourteen of them like barbecue beans, dirty rice, smoked potatoes and French fries. Standout desserts include the homemade sweet potato pie, gooey pecan pie or gluttonous golden deep fried Twinkie.

Chef Wayne's Big Mamou

63 Liberty St., Springfield, MA (413) 732-1011

www.chefwaynes-bigmamou.com

Chef Wayne's Big Mamou serves awesome Cajun and Creole cuisine in a friendly, fun space decked out in Louisiana murals and stuffed alligators. Enormous entrees include pork loin stuffed with cornbread, sage and sausage over rice. The house specialty blends crawfish, shrimp and veggies in a lobster brandy cream sauce with puff pastry. Spice it up with one of the hot sauces on the table and enjoy it with the beverage of your choice, because Wayne's is BYOB. Some customers even bring their own battery operated blenders for tableside margaritas. There's a second location with a full bar about thirty minutes north in Williamsburg.

Sonoma

206 Worcester Rd., Princeton, MA (978) 464-5775

www.sonomaprinceton.com

Sonoma is tucked away in the hills of Princeton, but it's worth seeking out for unforgettable global fare and an amazing California wine list. Silver vested servers are skilled at suggesting an oaky chardonnay or a crisp sauvignon blanc. At the end of the meal, they give every table a tour of the decadent dessert tray. All the original artwork is for sale, but Phantom suggests saving your pennies for exquisite dishes like the twin tournedos of filet mignon served with a truffle demi-glace or the roasted rack of lamb.

Antonio's Pizza

31 North Pleasant St., Amherst, MA (413) 253-0808

www.antoniospizza.com

Antonio's Pizza is a late night favorite for UMass students in search of a hot, cheesy slice of wildly creative pizza. Open until 2am on the weekends, college kids mob the counter in this tiny shop. Antonio's serves 200-300 kinds of pizza and about fifty exotic varieties are on display each day. Outrageous creations include the Beaurider with breaded chicken, tortellini and pesto. The Potato Bacon is loaded with butter, provolone, cheddar and rosemary. The Siracusa is stacked with sausage, caramelized onion, crème fraiche and blue cheese. There's even a steak burrito, steak taco or a steak quesadilla pizza. You can also get your slice fix at their stories in Easthampton and Providence.

The Federal

135 Cooper St., Agawam, MA (413) 789-1267

www.thefederalrestaurant.com

The Federal specializes in fine dining without the stuffiness. Lobster Shepherd's Pie, Chicken Bolognese and even house spun cotton candy are all on the menu. The playful "Bucket of Balls" features crispy arancini flavored with truffle oil. The Truffle Mac N Cheese is made with penne pasta, creamy Italian cheeses and black truffles (of course). Phantom's favorite dessert is the Peppermint S'mores

Cake made with chocolate cake, toasted menthol marshmallows and graham cracker crumble.

White Hut

280 Memorial Ave., West Springfield, MA (413) 736-9390

www.whitehut.com

Since 1939, White Hut has served simple, speedy, sensational hamburgers and hot dogs from a six hundred square foot spot. Burgers, dogs and fries are all you'll find on the menu. While everything is cooked to order, most diners are served in about three minutes. During the busy lunch rush, customers crowd the counter and stand five deep or more waiting for a chance to order. The burgers are two ounce patties of ninety percent lean ground sirloin. The quintessential White Hut meal is a cheeseburger with their famous "fried onions", cooked soft and sweet all day long. There are only a dozen counter seats and a small communal table, so while getting your food may be quick, finding a spot to dine may take some time. A brand new second location was recently opened in Amherst.

Rye & Thyme

14 Monument Sq., Leominster, MA (978) 534-5900

www.ryeandthyme.com

Housed in the historic Wood Block Building in downtown Leominster, Rye & Thyme has the charm of an old pub with modern features like a raw bar displaying an ever-changing selection of fresh oysters. The wood grill is responsible for cooking gourmet pizzas like the White with béchamel sauce, bacon, country ham and tomato garlic aioli. Carnivores will crave the cider brined thick-cut pork chop or the perfectly marbled Black Angus Delmonico. For dessert, the nostalgic Campfire Bread Pudding is a silky smooth blend of Belgian dark chocolate, marshmallows and vanilla ice cream. One extra bonus: the bartenders are extremely knowledgeable and they hand-craft some of the area's tastiest classic cocktails.

Chinatown
GREAT ATE

Shabu-Zen

16 Tyler St., Boston, MA (617) 292-8828
80 Brighton Ave., Allston, MA (617) 782-8888
www.shabuzen.com

Shabu-Zen is a bright, white walled room with tables around the periphery and a horseshoe of counter seats in the middle. Each table has individual, built-in hot pots for simmering food and chowing down. Like Japanese fondue, customers choose from a terrific selection of raw meats, veggies and seafood to cook tableside in bubbling broth. This Japanese hot pot cooking is called shabu-shabu, meaning "swish, swish". The name comes from the sound that's made from swirling thin, uncooked meats through a simmering pot of liquid. Generous entrees overflow with protein, vegetables, noodles, sauces and dessert. All of this fare pairs perfectly with Japanese sake, beer or wine. Customers can order a la carte, too.

Ginza

16 Hudson St., Boston, MA (617) 338-2261
www.ginza-boston.com

Ginza prepares awesome sushi and Japanese cuisine, staying open until 3:30am on the weekends. The dining room has bright, white walls and blond wood latticework, with elbow-to-elbow seating and a sushi bar toward the back. There's great people watching late at night when the clubbers and bar closers converge. The menu is packed with creative sushi options, thirteen kinds of sake and cooked Japanese dishes. All entrees include hot miso soup and a small iceberg lettuce salad with ginger dressing. There's a second location in Brookline.

Peach Farm

4 Tyler St., Boston, MA (617) 482-1116
www.peachfarmboston.com

Peach Farm is typical for what you find in Chinatown. The space is plain, with a few pieces of Chinese décor hung in the dining room. A tank at the entrance lets you know that the seafood is fresh. There are a few large circular tables for parties of eight to ten, so this is a great place to bring a group. Peach Farm is known for their authentic Cantonese style seafood with dishes like steamed sea bass or clams in black bean sauce. Soups, noodles and rice dishes are abundant and entrees include dishes like jumbo shrimp with walnuts and lobster with ginger and scallion. Peach Farm sometimes stays open until 3am for a post night out Chinese fix.

Dumpling Cafe

695 Washington St., Boston, MA (617) 338-8859

www.dumplingcafe.com

Even with tons of tables packed into the dining room, the Dumpling Cafe is always busy during meal times, particularly lunch. The space is a bit cleaner and newer than other places in the neighborhood. The menu is lined with Taiwanese fare, like Fried Stinky Tofu for the advanced eater and more user friendly options like crab rangoon and beef teriyaki. Most make the trip to the Dumpling Cafe for their famous soup dumplings. Presented in a bamboo steamer, these dumplings called "xiao long bao" have a doughy exterior with a pork meatball and hot broth inside. Eating your first one can get messy and even dangerous if the broth is hot enough, so take caution.

Q Restaurant

660 Washington St., Boston, MA (857) 350-3968

www.thequsa.com

Q Restaurant is a big, sexy space with high ceilings, huge windows and dim lighting. The contemporary style space has oversized booths that sit adjacent to a busy sushi bar rolling fresh maki that start at four bucks. Hot pot is their specialty with twelve broths and a long list of fish, meat and vegetables. Burners sit right in the tables so diners can have an interactive experience as they cook their own food. Q also has a big menu of hot Chinese specialties like Kung Pao Chicken, Beef and Broccoli and General Gau's Chicken.

Xinh Xinh

7 Beach St., Boston, MA (617) 422-0501

Xinh Xinh is a simple Vietnamese and Chinese restaurant with a few tables and very little to look at. What they lack in charming decor, they make up in charm with fast, friendly service. Dry erase boards list the daily specials. Phantom likes the pho, but before he starts his soup, he enjoys some of Xinh Xinh's fresh spring rolls served with a tasty peanut sauce for dipping. Other appetizers include beef or chicken teriyaki, fried chicken wings and Vietnamese style crepes. Big bowls of pho comes hot and steamy with the usual accompaniments. Order some bubble tea to make the experience even sweeter.

Jade Garden

18-20 Tyler St., Boston, MA (617) 423-3288

Jade Garden is one of the few stylish restaurants in Chinatown with flat screens on the wall and fish tanks filled with fresh selections. The spacious dining room is full of customers feasting on typical Chinese fare like lobster with ginger and sizzling chicken, plus unique offerings like the Hong Kong Steak slathered in a tasty brown sauce or the flavorful Salt and Pepper Fried Pork Chops. Phantom always gets an order of the fried dumplings, cooked perfectly brown on the outside and hot and steamy in the center, served with a soy ginger dipping sauce. Hit this place for lunch when you can get a satisfying meal for under five bucks.

China King

60 Beach St., Boston, MA (617) 542-1763

China King serves some of Chinatown's most authentic Chinese in a plain red walled dining room with hanging paper lanterns. To start, order the Peking ravioli stuffed with pork. The Shanghai Chow Mein is a must try, stir-fried with pork and cabbage. Full of thick, house made noodles, this is easily one of the best dishes not just in Chinatown, but in all of Boston. The Peking Duck meal may be the best thing on the menu, but it requires twenty-four hour advance notice. It's served in three courses starting with accompaniments including pancakes, hoisin and scallions. The second course brings a stir-fry, followed by soup. A note for the squeamish: The duck is presented to the table with its head on ready for carving.

East Boston
GREAT ATE

Angela's Cafe

131 Lexington St., East Boston, MA (617) 567-4972

www.angelascaferestaurant.com

Angela's is a tiny, corner Mexican eatery in a mostly residential neighborhood. A nondescript hole-in-the-wall from the outside, the cheery interior is decked out with colorful paper cutouts, hot pink curtains and festive decorations dangling from the ceiling. The appealing menu forgoes the usual Americanized Tex-Mex in favor of authentic south-of-the-border cuisine. A sharable start to your meal is the Favoritos de Angela, a great sampler platter with tacos, tostadas and gorditas. Phantom loves washing it down with a pitcher of house made sangria. Single digit starters and entrees in the teens make for a truly frugal fiesta.

D'Amelio's Off the Boat

26 Porter St., East Boston, MA (617) 561-8800

www.offtheboatseafood.com

There's no place better for homestyle Italian and ultra-fresh seafood than D'Amelio's Off the Boat. This casual Eastie eatery started as a small takeout shop that became so popular, D'Amelio's had to create the intimate dining room next door. While the space may be small, the dishes are huge. From the name, it's obvious that seafood is their specialty with dishes like the frutti di mare or the oversized fried Fisherman's Platter. There's also juicy chicken parm and tender Veal Marsala. Finish your Off the Boat experience with the Chocolate Bomba from the dessert menu, a veritable bocce ball of ice cream wrapped in a hard chocolate shell.

Kelley's Square Pub

84 Bennington St., East Boston, MA (617) 567-4627

www.kelleyssquarepub.com

Kelley's Square Pub is a neighborhood favorite lined with locals watching sports at the bar and families filling the dining room for hearty portions at pocket friendly prices. Regulars rave about the charbroiled steak tips and the satisfying sausage. However, Phantom is a fiend for their pizzas because they're tasty and inexpensive, with the large cheese being the ultimate value at less than ten bucks.

The shrimp scampi pizza is probably the most popular and sometimes can be smelled from streets away. There are a few parking spaces in the back, so check there first before circling the block.

Sonny Noto's

22 Central Sq., East Boston, MA (617) 569-1993

49 Water St., Wakefield, MA (781) 246-4800

www.sonnynotos.com

This cafeteria-style Eastie eatery has been around for forty-five years, with a newer location in Wakefield. Phantom loves chowing down on The Noto Special: a sub comprised of fried chicken cutlets, slices of prosciutto, fresh buffalo mozzarella and roasted red peppers. Just as tasty is the steak and cheese made with lean, shaved steak that's grilled, smothered with American cheese and flipped directly into a fresh baked sub roll. The steak tips are Phan favorites, soaked in a tangy, sweet, top-secret Asian-style marinade. No matter what you get, you're bound to require a takeout box as the portions are so big, they're nearly impossible to finish in one sitting.

Royal Roast Beef & Seafood

752 Bennington St., East Boston, MA (617) 567-7779

www.royalroastbeef.com

This family owned and operated restaurant has been serving Eastie for over twenty years. Situated opposite of Constitution Beach, Royal is a small, casual counter service eatery that serves food fast that would never be called "fast food". Open late, Royal is a good spot to hit on your way home from a night out. Fried clams, shrimp and scallops come fresh off the boat and are cooked until golden and crispy. For the royal treatment at Royal, order a thin sliced roast beef sandwich. The "Super Beef" is served on a toasted onion roll and it's best when ordered "three way": BBQ sauce, cheese and mayonnaise.

Italian Express

336 Sumner St., East Boston, MA (617) 561-0038

www.italianexpresspizzeria.com

Tucked in a residential part of East Boston, Italian Express is a casual restaurant featuring a menu lined with old family recipes passed down through generations. The meatballs are legendary and slow cooked in marinara until they're moist. You can order veal, chicken or shrimp prepared one of ten ways, including cacciatore, limone, Marsala and fra diavolo. Pizzas are enormous and served perched on large Pastene cans. You may even run into Boston Mayor Tom Menino, who frequents this place so much, they named the Rolled Eggplant Menino after him.

Roy's Cold Cuts

198 Marion St., East Boston, MA (617) 567-9760

Roy's Cold Cuts is a quirky sub shop serving some serious sandwiches. When you walk into Roy's, you'll feel like you walked into the Rock and Roll Hall of Fame as this takeout only shop is full of 60's and 70's music memorabilia. As for the food, the Godfather is packed with a crispy chicken cutlet, Parma prosciutto, fresh mozzarella, roasted peppers and tomato. The Royben, Roy's twist on the classic Reuben, is layered with perfectly cooked corned beef smothered in 1000 Island dressing and topped with Swiss. Don't leave without picking up a few of Roy's nostalgic candies lined across the wall.

Dough

20 Maverick St., East Boston, MA (617) 567-8787

www.doughpizza.com

Dough looks like a typical Eastie sub shop with limited seating, but the premium sandwiches are a step above the rest. The Reuben burger marries the deli classic to the fast food favorite and the amped up grilled cheese is loaded with Swiss, mozzarella, provolone and cheddar. The Vermonter is made so meticulously, the menu asks to "allow ten minutes for construction". This sandwich is a mouthful, piled high with maple turkey, chopped bacon, red onion, green apples and smoked Gouda on two thick slices of multigrain bread with sundried tomato mayo. Pizza is just as tasty and includes creative options like the Hawaiian with prosciutto, pineapple and toasted coconut or the Orchard, a surprisingly addictive combination of chicken, bacon, onions and apples.

Fenway
GREAT ATE

La Verdad

1 Lansdowne St., Boston, MA (617) 351-2580

www.laverdadtaqueria.com

La Verdad provides cantina style Mexican street food to pre-game Red Sox fans and a lively crowd year round. With bright colors and even more vibrant fare, La Verdad is a fiesta. Chef Ken Oringer, normally known for his upscale cooking at places like Clio, Coppa and Toro, makes user friendly dishes like tender steak quesadillas, chicken burritos, queso fundido with chorizo, and nachos piled with the good stuff. The tacos are the most authentic in Greater Boston, stuffed with Ensenada style fried fish, chipotle stewed chicken and ancho braised short ribs. For the more adventurous palates, La Verdad has creative fare like lamb enchiladas.

Audubon Circle

838 Beacon St., Boston, MA (617) 421-1910

www.auduboncircle.us

Audubon Circle is a stylish urban space with a sleek slate bar, raised tables, massive blackboard menus and warm wood paneling. It draws an eclectic crowd where college kids feel sophisticated, seasoned drinkers feel cool, and Red Sox fans can commiserate. The menu is more cafe comfort food than pub grub with fancy pressed sandwiches, signature salads and a few upscale entrees. Wide-mouth burgers come with well-done roasted potatoes cooked until the seasoned skin turns crunchy brown. The pork potstickers come in a fun takeout container tossed with sautéed peapods, water chestnuts, red bell pepper and pretty lotus root. Audubon Circle is practically pitching distance from Fenway Park, so parking can be tough.

Sweet Caroline's Restaurant & Bar

1260 Boylston St., Boston, MA (617) 424-1260

www.sweetcarolinesboston.com

New to the neighborhood, Sweet Caroline's is the ultimate spot for pregame snacks and suds. While it's loud and fun with plenty of flat screens, there's something a bit more refined about this "sports bar". The space is open and airy and a visually stunning wall acts as a "live green monster" with greenery planted vertically. The perfect starter is the customizable appetizer platter where diners choose four selections like Buffalo chicken rangoons or steak and cheese eggrolls for just over thirty bucks. There are six bountiful burgers and hearty entrees like lobster stuffed haddock or tender, juicy steak tips. Phantom doesn't leave without ordering the Fresh Baked Cookie Dough Pie. It's baked in a personal skillet and topped with vanilla ice cream, whipped cream and chocolate sauce.

Citizen Public House & Oyster Bar

1310 Boylston St., Boston, MA (617) 450-9000

www.citizenpub.com

The Citizen is a dark, cozy nook shucking some of the city's freshest oysters. It's a low key spot with hip music and a fireplace crackling during the cooler months. While the oysters are the draw, Phantom loves nothing more than their Peel N' Eat Shrimp studded with Old Bay seasoning. For something more substantial, try the Citizen Carpetbagger. This throwback dish consists of a ten ounce filet topped with oyster compound butter and a fried oyster. Large parties should consider pre-booking a family style pig roast. The bartenders take their drinks so seriously, they even offer special oversized ice balls for certain drinks.

Bleacher Bar

82 Lansdowne St., Boston, MA (617) 262-2424

www.bleacherbarboston.com

The Bleacher Bar on Landsdowne is literally attached to Fenway Park. The restaurant is below the bleachers and a special screen lets fan see directly into center field. There's no cover to get in, just a request to rotate seats from time to time. Flatbreads can be topped with everything from cheese steak to pastrami. Sliders comes in three different forms: burger, sausage and pastrami. Snacks to share over some beers include gravy fries, onion rings with spicy ranch, fried pickles and stuffed cherry peppers.

The Sausage Guy

49 Lansdowne St., Boston, MA (617) 268-8324

www.sausageguy.com

The Sausage Guy (aka David Littlefield) is as much a Boston institution as the Green Monster, and he sets up his world famous sausage cart just behind Fenway's famous wall on Lansdowne Street. The sausages feature a special blend of Italian seasonings so they're not too sweet and not too spicy. Sauteed peppers and onions are slathered right on top, stacked in a nice fluffy sub roll and served incredibly fast for a fraction of the price you'd pay inside the ballpark. This is also a popular attraction for a late night snack when the bars and clubs let out for the Kenmore crowds.

Petit Robert Bistro

468 Commonwealth Ave., Boston, MA (617) 375-0699

www.petiterobertbistro.com

Petit Robert Bistro is a bi-level, brick-walled eatery evoking a proper Parisian setting of mirrors, blackboards, candles and an open kitchen. Downstairs at the dessert bar, the pastry chef puts on a sugary show, plating all the sweet sensations before your eyes. The French onion soup is a savory beginning, presented in a crock sealed with oven-browned cheese. The mussels are drenched in a white wine shallot broth you'll want to mop up with bread. The Boeuf Bourguignon is a hearty dish that will fill you as it warms you in the colder months. Brunch is served every day of the week with outstanding omelettes, quiche and savory crepes. There are additional locations in the South End, Brighton and Needham.

The Hawthorne

500A Commonwealth Ave., Boston, MA (617) 532-9150

www.thehawthornebar.com

Inside the Hotel Commonwealth, the Hawthorne is a posh spot serving craft cocktails with a small but impressive bar menu. A long bar sits at the back of the room with several clusters of couches to sip drinks with friends. Some snacks for sharing include soft pretzels served with a bourbon mustard, deviled eggs with crispy prosciutto and tiny Reubens made on small pieces of toast with barrel-aged kraut. For something more substantial to soak up the spirits, there's a glorified grilled cheese made with creamy robiola and Dijon, fingerling potato skins stuffed with raclette, bacon and horseradish cream, and a satisfying steak salad topped with Stilton and shallot vinaigrette.

Merrimack Valley
GREAT ATE

Yella

16 Post Office Ave., Andover, MA (978) 749-0011

www.yellagrille.com

Yella is a small, romantic spot run by a young husband/wife team. Danielle and Carlo Berdahn have created a stylish space with huge windows and candle light, giving their guests a real feeling of comfort. Lebanese recipes that have been passed down from Carlo's mother line the menu. Some of his specialties include pan seared salmon, a grilled ribeye with wild mushrooms and plump sea scallops over truffled risotto. Believe it or not, the most popular item is Yella's crispy chicken wings. These aren't like anything you'd find in a sports bar, soaked in garlicky extra virgin olive oil with lemon and tomato.

Aprile's European Restaurant

75 Princeton St., North Chelmsford, MA (978) 455-3111

www.aprileseuropeanrestaurant.com

Aprile's is a spinoff of the European, a restaurant everybody knew and loved in the North End. While this location most definitely doesn't look like Hanover Street, with its sprawling dining room and floor to ceiling windows overlooking a stream, it sure does taste like the old European right down to the famously oversized pizzas. As for the Italian entrees, the Brogliamenti includes chicken parm, eggplant parm, ravioli, meatballs, sausage, veal marsala and sautéed spinach. The dish is made for two but can easily feed four. Prices are more than reasonable with appetizers averaging less than ten bucks and most entrees under twenty.

Krueger Flatbread

142 Essex St., Haverhill, MA (978) 372-3434

www.kruegerflatbread.com

At Krueger Flatbread, inside the old Krueger Brewery in downtown Haverhill, they're re-inventing pizza. The dough is the secret, sweetened with a touch of honey. A wood-fired five hundred degree pizza oven is right in the dining room, so you have a front row seat for all the action. Creative pizza combos include fire roasted steak tips, caramelized onions and crumbled blue cheese. Everything you'd expect to see stuffed in a taco is on the Tex Mex pizza. Krueger's top selling flatbread is still the plain cheese. But, those in the know always go for something a little more special, like the Chicken Marsala flatbread. It's a true Krueger original, topped with an entire Chicken Marsala dinner from the kitchen of their sister restaurant Olivia's right next door.

Skip's Snack Bar

92 East Main St., Merrimac, MA (978) 346-8686

There are thousands of ways to slice a spud, but no one does it quite like Skip's Snack Bar. Since 1947, this Merrimac mainstay has cranked out millions of pounds of their signature Suzie Q Potato. Shaped like a spiral phone cord, the curly Suzie Q has been made the same way, on the same hand-powered slicers, for sixty years. While most of the curls are eight inches long, the record is a whopping sixteen feet made from one giant spud. The 50's-themed quick stop makes other fast food too, including grilled hot dogs, turkey clubs and chicken fingers. Phantom's favorite is the Angus beef double cheeseburger. This may be called a "snack bar", but there's plenty of seating to eat your food on-site. Skip's is cash only and open seasonally from April until early October.

AJ's Kitchen

162 Lowell St., Wilmington, MA (978) 657-0037

www.ajskitchen.net

At AJ's Kitchen, a family of four can eat a complete meal for less than twenty-five dollars. This mostly takeout spot has a few tables for indoor dining. Every oversized, overstuffed sub and sandwich is served on freshly baked bread still warm out of the oven. The Roast Beef Melt is a cheesy dream on toasted scali. The Italian sub is absolutely loaded with cold cuts and fresh veggies. But, the real specialty is the meatball sub served on a gigantic braided sub roll. The calzones are even more impressive. These two feet monstrosities pack enough stuff to fill three subs. Whether you order the gut-busting chicken parm calzone or the best-selling Italian, every toasty, doughy delight is brushed with a buttery garlic sauce to keep the bread soft and the flavor kicking.

Ceia Kitchen + Bar

25 State St., Newburyport, MA (978) 358-8112

www.ceia-newburyport.com

An intimate nook in the downtown area, Ceia serves Portuguese cuisine with a twist. While the fare may be upscale, there's nothing pretentious about the atmosphere with friendly service and a laid back attitude. The scratch kitchen makes everything fresh daily. There's rich Lobster Gnocchi with saffron and the fragrant, flavor-packed Shrimp Mozambique with roasted garlic crostini. A non-traditional dish that has regulars raving is Ceia's Kobe beef and Manchego cheese burger served with crispy sweet potato fries. The perfect way to end any meal at Ceia is the Banana Brulee, featuring a torched clove meringue with bananas and crushed hazelnuts.

Pub 97

935 Salem St., Groveland, MA (978) 372-3320

www.pub97.webs.com

At Pub 97, they don't just serve a few specialty burgers. They offer ninety-seven char-grilled, half pound Angus burgers. This come as you are watering hole has a bar full of locals polishing off burgers and beers alongside a dining room with games for the kids. There's the Polynesian Burger with sweet and sour sauce, pepper jack cheese and crushed pineapple. The Surf and Turf Burger is topped with four juicy grilled shrimp. The carb friendly "Inside Out" consists of one half of a bun placed between two burgers. If you want to make a little hamburger history, put on your loose fitting pants and order The Challenge Burger: a six patty burger served with three pounds of fries. Eat it in an hour, and it's free. Plus you get a twenty-five dollar gift certificate for your next visit.

Vic's

1 Lilley Ave., Lowell, MA (978) 458-2021

www.vicspizzasubs.com

Vic's has served huge portions at tiny prices since 1962. This place is like three different businesses under one roof. There's a sub shop attached to a bakery attached to a diner. The sub shop claims it's the "Home of the Big One", where a large sub measures eighteen inches long, weighs more than two pounds and costs less than ten bucks. Vic's hundred seat diner serves breakfast seven days a week. The Lumberjack is enough for breakfast and lunch with two giant pancakes, two eggs, three strips of bacon, three sausages, homefries and toast. Down the hall in the bakery, everything is made by hand, from the brownies and whoopie pies to the fruit packed apple squares.

MetroWest
GREAT ATE

Oregon Club

117 Oregon Rd., Ashland, MA (508) 875-9030

www.theoregonclubofashland.com

Once a speakeasy and now a cozy dining spot, the Oregon Club is located in a ninety year old house and serves classic American cuisine. In addition to the Club's signature spicy mushroom soup, the menu includes homemade veal meatballs, barbecue spare ribs, creamy fettuccine Bolognese and crispy duck confit. The dish that made the Oregon Club famous is the sirloin steak that's seared in beef fat. It's crunchy on the outside, with a perfectly cooked center that will melt in your mouth. In the dining room, you'll find walls lined with photos of prominent club members from the past including clergymen, doctors, judges, and even Red Sox legend Ted Williams.

Tomasso Trattoria

154 Turnpike Rd., Southborough, MA (508) 481-8484

www.tomassotrattoria.com

Tomasso Trattoria is a handsome space of wide striped floors and ceiling arches wrapped in earth tones. Acorn lanterns stretch the wine bar and kitchen counter seats, and suburbanites relax into leather booths and spread out tables. The traditional Italian menu is rich with exciting wines, antipasti for mixing and matching, house made pasta and rustic entrees. Dishes are served small, as they are in Italy, so you can easily eat a few delicious courses. Phantom loves to finish his meal with Tomasso's authentic vanilla bean gelato.

Coach Grill

55 Boston Post Rd., Wayland, MA (508) 358-5900

www.coachgrillrestaurant.com

The Coach Grill is an upscale steak house with a masculine dark wood interior of curved black leather banquettes, mirrored walls and equestrian art. Stone fireplaces flank the lively rooms and stately lamps suspend from recessed ceilings. Sophisticated servers wear tan butcher jackets and deliver smooth service with rolling cart presentation of each course. The meaty menu includes steaks aged for five weeks, plus chops, seafood, rotisserie selections and a fine wine list. True to steak house form, portions of sides and sweets come oversized in sharable a la carte orders. Since its sister restaurant is Abe & Louie's, you know they're worth their salt when it comes to steak.

Aegean

257 Cochituate Rd., Framingham, MA (508) 879-8424

640 Arsenal St., Watertown, MA (617) 923-7771

www.aegeanrestaurants.com

The Aegean is a sprawling Greek restaurant featuring an expansive menu loaded with outstanding value. Each meal begins with complimentary pita bread with an olive oil and feta cheese dip. Appetizers include the golden, flaky spinach and cheese pies or the shrimp saganaki sautéed with garlic, tomatoes and feta. Entrees like the tender, marinated lamb chops or the seafood platter packed with haddock, sole, salmon, scallops and baked stuffed shrimp come with a Greek salad. Desserts cover the classics, like sticky-sweet baklava and the creamy, custard-filled galaktoboureko.

Ten-Ichi

1400 Worcester St., Natick, MA (508) 875-1888

www.tenichidkb.com

Ten-Ichi on Route 9 is a state of the art Asian restaurant with three distinct dining options: sushi, hot pot, and dim sum. The tables at Ten-Ichi features a high-tech induction cooker that gets the hot pot boiling in seconds. It comes with a variety of fresh vegetables and your choice of thinly sliced meats like short ribs, white meat chicken or assorted seafood you cook to your liking right at the table. The sushi menu has an astounding variety of fresh, beautifully prepared fish. Dim sum like the Shanghai style soup dumplings and fluffy roast pork buns are hand-crafted and served in bamboo steamers.

Prime 131 Grill

131 Boston Post Rd., Wayland, MA (508) 358-2400

www.prime131.com

More than just another steak house and beyond your basic cocktail lounge, Prime 131 Grill has all the style and sizzle you'd expect to find in a big city. The bar is always busy and the kitchen specializes in hand-selected steaks. There are classic steak house appetizers like bacon-wrapped scallops in a Chambord maple glaze. The six ounce filet mignon comes wrapped in bacon in a port demi-glace. There are also more down home menu items like the mouthwatering burger topped with Monterey Jack cheese, smoked applewood bacon and sauteed mushrooms or the satisfying lobster B.L.T. For dessert, the deliciously explosive Avalanche Sundae is topped with caramel sauce, roasted pecans and whipped cream.

Arturo's

54 East Main St., Westboro, MA (508) 366-1881

www.arturosristorante.com

Arturo's hand crafts classic Italian food made great from generations of practice. You can always find chef/owner Domenico Fabiano in the kitchen cooking old family recipes like parpadelle Bolognese, garlicky shrimp scampi and lobster ravioli in a shallot sherry cream sauce. Appetizers include crunchy bruschetta and antipasto for two with grilled vegetables, sliced imported prosciutto, sopressata, Cacio di Roma cheese and house made mozzarella. Thin crust pizzas are made simple with the freshest ingredients. Entrees include the San Marzano Chicken served in a sun-dried tomato cream sauce. The frutti di mare is a generous portion of fresh seafood and pasta, and for a classic Italian feast, order the spaghetti and meatballs.

Marathon Restaurant at North Pond

25 Hayward St., Hopkinton, MA (508) 589-6400

www.themarathonrestaurant.com

Marathon Restaurant is an upscale American bistro with a bar downstairs and a comfortable dining room upstairs. Named for the Boston Marathon that starts at the town green, Marathon serves the kind of food that will make you want to run to the restaurant. For those wanting to load up on carbs, there are pasta dishes like chicken broccoli and penne, lobster ravioli or mac and cheese. Juicy burgers can be customized with twenty toppings. There's the simple grilled margherita pizza or the more sophisticated Alsatian pizza, topped with crème fraiche, ricotta, smoked bacon, caramelized onions and mozzarella. If that doesn't fill you up, the dense Flourless Chocolate Torte with Grand Marnier and raspberry coulis will.

New Hampshire
GREAT ATE

Copper Door

15 Leavy Dr., Bedford, NH (603) 488-2677

www.copperdoorrestaurant.com

The Copper Door serves upscale comfort food with a New American twist. The open and airy dining rooms have soaring ceilings, wooden beams, and local art. There's a large and happening bar mixing creative cocktails alongside an extensive wine list. Appetizers include Tenderloin Sliders with caramelized onion and gorgonzola fondue, Bacon Wrapped Shrimp with wild honey, and Steak and Cheese Spring Rolls with spicy ketchup. Traditional favorites are well represented like bacon topped meatloaf with mushroom gravy and onion straws and the buttermilk fried chicken with garlic mashed potatoes.

Hart's Turkey Farm

233 Daniel Webster Hwy., Meredith, NH (603) 279-6212

www.hartsturkeyfarm.com

Every day is Thanksgiving Day at Hart's Turkey Farm. The gigantic, casual space is open and bright with wood paneling and a prevalent turkey theme. The menu is lined with poultry favorites like turkey croquettes, turkey livers, turkey pie, turkey sandwiches, turkey burgers, turkey nuggets and turkey soup. The Turkey Plate comes in three sizes, including "jumbo" with over a pound of hand carved turkey, gravy, stuffing and cranberry sauce. If turkey isn't your thing, Hart's offers plenty of alternatives like succulent steak tips, fresh seafood and loads of sandwiches and salads.

Parker's Maple Barn

1316 Brookline Rd., Mason, NH (603) 878-2308

www.parkersmaplebarn.com

Parker's Maple Barn is a backwoods treasure where you can see the maple syrup being made before you sample the sweet stuff over a hearty breakfast. The restaurant was converted out of a 19th century barn and boasts a full menu including seven kinds of pancakes and maple glazed baby back ribs. During the season, customers can take a tour of the sweet-smelling adjacent Sugar House.

Inexpensive portions are fit for a lumberjack, and the house maple syrup flows in unlimited supply. There's an on-site gift shop where all the maple products can be purchased to take home. Parker's is closed in January.

Tuscan Kitchen

67 Main St., Salem, NH (603) 952-4875

www.tuscan-kitchen.com

Tuscan Kitchen is a gorgeous two floor restaurant, fashioned after an Italian farmhouse. Every meal starts with a basket of warm ciabatta and focaccia served with Sicilian olive oil and aged balsamic. Appetizers include crispy golden Lobster Arancini, wonderful meatballs with Parmesan fonduta, and wood oven pizzas cooked until crispy. Pastas like Lobster Ravioli, Tagliatelle Bolognese and Potato Gnocchi are all made on-site. Phantom loves the Roasted Butternut Squash Cappellacci with a sage brown butter sauce. Carnivores will crave the twenty-eight ounce sea salt and rosemary crusted bone-in ribeye. For a truly over the top experience, nothing beats the two pound, slow braised osso bucco with saffron risotto and root vegetables.

MT's Local

212 Main St., Nashua, NH (603) 595-9334

www.mtslocal.com

MT's Local is a casual but chic eatery with a bustling quasi-open kitchen and a lively bar. The menu is lined with casual fare like burgers, ribs, and wood grilled pizzas. Diners can have a more upscale experience with entrees like the Citrus Pressed Chicken marinated with rosemary, garlic, and lemon quick cooked in a 500 degree cast iron pan. Phantom's favorite dish is the signature Bistro Beef Tournedos, a pair of wood grilled tenderloin medallions served on garlic crostini with grilled tomato, crispy pancetta, and spinach Hollandaise that combine into a symphony of flavors.

Lobster Q

416 Emerson Ave., Hampstead, NH (603) 329-4094

www.lobsterq.com

Even though this quirky, family friendly restaurant is in a strip mall, it offers quality fare in a casual atmosphere with an enthusiastic owner. The kitchen specializes in two things: lobster and barbecue. Lobster comes boiled, stuffed in a lobster roll, or served on top of a salad. The BBQ side of the menu brings slow-smoked ribs and Southern style pulled pork. While Phantom loves lobster and barbecue, he finds the King's Haddock hard to resist. This fresh fish filet is wrapped around a sumptuous seafood stuffing, baked and then smothered in a creamy lobster bisque.

Woodstock Station

135 Main St., North Woodstock, NH (800) 321-3985

www.woodstockinnnh.com

Located in the heart of the White Mountains, the Woodstock Station is housed in an old train depot and features a dining room filled with railroad memorabilia and wacky signs. You'll also find plenty of satisfied customers feasting on plates that come in one size, huge. The menu is just as big, offering pizza, sandwiches, steak, seafood, salads and the heart-stopping "Death by Burger". This jaw breaker features an eighteen ounce cheeseburger on the bottom and an entire BLT on the top. After a meal like that, you'll be glad the restaurant is housed on the grounds of the Woodstock Inn with thirty-three comfortable guest rooms to spend the night. There's also a working brewery for beer lovers to take a tour and sip samples.

The Common Man

88 Range Rd., Windham, NH (603) 898-0088

www.thecman.com

The Common Man is a unique New Hampshire chain with rustic, charming locations. They're incredibly cozy with stone fireplaces, a lodge-like bar and enough antiques to make a museum. The experience starts with free cheese and crackers and progresses to creative, eclectic cuisine that draws from local produce, fish, and meat. Inventive appetizers include Caribbean Jerk wings or the Brie Stuffed Portobello. For entrees, the Mixed Grill is three dishes in one, combining a steak fillet, chicken smothered in blueberry-honey sauce, and a crab cake with horseradish mayo. Desserts might be the best thing on the menu. There's a smothered brownie sundae and the Uncommon Baked Apple coated in maple syrup and brown sugar, served with homemade ice cream.

Carmen

33 North Sq., Boston, MA (617) 742-6421

www.carmenboston.com

Carmen is a closet sized North End eatery with a snug dining area that's just a little bigger than the mini bar up front. Rough brick walls, wine racks on display, dim lighting and fresh flowers add up to romantic ambiance, but clubby music lightens the mood. The Italian menu starts with small tapas style plates followed by a limited choice of pasta and entrees. The dish to order is the baked penne prepared in parchment paper with Apulian-style, parsley flecked meatballs, melted mozzarella and chunky roasted tomato sauce. There isn't dessert, but in a neighborhood filled with bakeries you don't have to go far to find something sweet.

Strega

379 Hanover St., Boston, MA (617) 523-8481

www.stregaristorante.com

Straying from red sauce tradition, Strega gives the North End creative Italian cooking and glittery décor that draws celebrities. The restaurant's name means "witch" in Italian, and the hypnotizing theme translates into vivid wall murals. The look is racy and hot, with flirtatious yellow backlighting to illuminate the room's royal colors and stylish black clad servers. Mob movies like The Godfather play on the flat screen TVs, but all eyes are on the modern Italian dishes like Fettuccine Strega with shrimp, scallops and baby spinach in a light cream sauce made with Strega liquor. Phantom loves the homemade mozzarella and the lightly fried calamari.

Galleria Umberto

289 Hanover St., Boston, MA (617) 227-5709

Galleria Umberto is hit hard during lunch, which is the only meal served. The doors of the cafeteria-style eatery stay open until the food runs out, which doesn't take long because this is one of the busiest lunch spots in Boston. Although the menu is limited, you won't find better Sicilian specialties anywhere. Phantom likes to line up early for four kinds of calzones filled with combinations of ricotta, mozzarella, spinach, salami, and sausage. Square Sicilian-style slices of pizza come on a thick crust, and deep fried arancini rice balls hide a cache of peas and gravy. The price is right, with a full lunch costing way less than $10. You can also order tiny Dixie cups of table wine.

Neptune Oyster

63 Salem St., Boston, MA (617) 742-3474

www.neptuneoyster.com

Shucking its way to the top, Neptune Oyster is the freshest raw bar around and a very unusual spot for the North End. The attractive clam shack sized room has all the luster of a South Pacific pearl. Three dozen seats hug the long marble bar, trimmed in vintage mirrors and set off by a textured tin ceiling. There's a big selection of raw items like iced scallops, oysters and littleneck clams. Giving a nod to the neighborhood, the kitchen also turns out Italian seafood like lobster cioppino, fried calamari, and shellfish stew with saffron rice.

Giacomo's

355 Hanover St., Boston, MA (617) 523-9026

431 Columbus Ave., Boston (617) 536-5723

Giacomo's is a comfortable everyday eatery with one tiny brick room that's practically in the kitchen. Copper pots hang above the stove and forty seats are squeezed into the small space. A huge blackboard menu lists basic Italian fare, with five essential sauces, lots of pasta and plenty of seafood. Appetizers include the incredibly light fried calamari with jalapeno accents. There are typical North End plates like veal parm, chicken marsala and shrimp scampi. Big, heaping portions are as consistent as the snaking line of hungry customers out the door. Like many of its neighbors, Giacomo's doesn't serve dessert, leaving sweets and coffee to the many pastry experts on the street. This is a cash only establishment with a second location in the South End.

Ristorante Saraceno

286 Hanover St., Boston, MA (617) 227-5888

www.saracenos.com

Saraceno has been a landmark on Hanover Street for over twenty-five years. From the outside it looks tiny, but inside there are three levels full of old world style eats served in a homey dining room with Italian inspired art throughout. Popular dishes include Spaghetti Amatriciana with homemade pasta, pancetta, onions and sharp Parmesan cheese or the gigantic plate of Frutti di Mare overflowing with fresh scallops, shrimp, mussels and clams in a light tomato sauce over linguini. Lobster is also prepared boiled, grilled or in a spicy red sauce.

Enoteca Bricco

241 Hanover St., Boston, MA (617) 248-6800

www.bricco.com

Enoteca Bricco is a North End wine bar with candlelit dining, big open windows and handsome two toned wood floors. Each tightly positioned table has a great view of the exhibition kitchen, with its wood burning oven and dangling copper pots. The modern Italian menu boasts house made pastas and steaks (beautifully seared then grilled) that rival some of best in the city. Artisanal pastas include gnocchi with bufala mozzarella, tomatoes and basil and pumpkin tortelli served in truffle honey and sage butter. Entrees include chicken "under a brick" prepared in a seven spice marinade and a tender veal osso bucco. For serious seafood lovers, Phantom suggests Bricco's Brodetto which includes one half lobster, calamari, swordfish, monkfish, Wellfleet clams and mussels.

Mare

135 Richmond St., Boston, MA (617) 723-6273

www.marenatural.com

Mare Oyster Bar may be in the North End, but this isn't your run of the mill red sauce joint. Located on the corner of Richmond and North Streets, this elegant eatery has floor to ceiling windows for people watching in Boston's oldest neighborhood. The menu takes full advantage of its proximity to the ocean by serving fresh seafood like the shellfish tower: a two tiered selection of fresh oysters, crab, clams, shrimp and lobster on ice. There's a larger than life Maine lobster packed with savory seafood stuffing. The lobster roll is special because the brioche bun is baked fresh daily. That same buttery brioche is also used on Mare's burger, topped with cheddar, bacon and Parmesan aioli.

The Blue Ox

191 Oxford St., Lynn, MA (781) 780-5722

www.theblueoxlynn.com

The Blue Ox seems more like it's in downtown Boston than downtown Lynn. This upscale neighborhood eatery has blue walls, cool paintings and tasty, affordable American cuisine. Appetizers include unexpected dishes like tuna tartare with chive cream and homemade chips or the creamy baked Brie stuffed with apricots, figs and cranberries. Heavier meals include large plates of gnocchi Bolognese or the pork tenderloin made with an apple cider reduction and mashed sweet potatoes. There are sophisticated dishes like the wild mushroom ravioli with brown butter and more casual fare like the duo of Blue Ox Burgers, stuffed with blue cheese and topped with apple wood smoked bacon served alongside hand cut rosemary and parsley fries.

New Brothers

31 Maple St., Danvers, MA (978) 750-0100

www.newbrothersdanvers.com

New Brothers is set up like a classic cafeteria with big menu boards, plenty of seat yourself tables and a lineup of piping hot daily specials for less than ten dollars. Breakfast is the most popular meal of the day, featuring corned beef hash, golden French toast, fluffy pancakes, and mounds of breakfast potatoes served hot off the grill. At lunch and dinner, there are perfectly executed Reuben sandwiches stacked with piles of corned beef and Greek specialties like moussaka. You can get a Greek salad topped with big blocks of feta and char-grilled steak tips or a generous Caesar salad served in a tortilla bowl. The chicken kebobs are big enough for two meals and the house-roasted turkey dinner is Thanksgiving-worthy any day of the year.

Barking Dog

21 Friend St., Amesbury, MA (978) 388-9537

www.barkingdoggrill.com

This no-fuss restaurant is a local favorite where hefty portions are served under white Christmas lights and funky stained glass windows. Appetizers include a pinwheel of grilled kielbasa with Dijon mustard. The "Barking Mac and Cheese" is baked with buttery Ritz crackers overflowing with pasta and cheddar. The ten ounce Angus burger stands dangerously tall, as does the "Barking BLT" stacked to the ceiling on toasty bread. The Barking Dog's biggest seller is the chicken salad sandwich. It's stuffed inside a toasted pita with plenty of pesto dressing. For dessert, the Cinnamon Bun Sundae demands attention with three huge scoops of vanilla ice cream nestled on a warm cinnamon roll and drizzled with caramel sauce and powdered sugar.

Brenden Crocker's Wild Horse Cafe

392 Cabot St., Beverly, MA (978) 922-6868

www.wildhorsecafe.com

Brenden Crocker's Wild Horse Cafe is the kind of restaurant where you can go for a romantic date night, a fun night of drinking or a roll-up-your-sleeves and chow down night on the town. The atmosphere is all about comfort, with plush couches and oversized chairs. The grassroots cuisine is cooked perfectly and served in truly enormous portions. From the famous bar nachos, to pistachio crusted sea scallops, to the Wild Horse cheese fondue, the menu goes hand-in-hand with the extensive craft beer and cocktail list. You can usually spot Brenden himself by the wood-burning oven and grill, firing filet mignon with roasted root vegetables, twelve ounce burgers topped with bacon and mushrooms or even a Wood Grilled Banana with warm homemade caramel.

Great Escape

50 Saint Peter St., Salem, MA (978) 745-5022

www.greatescaperest.com

Great Escape is perched high on a hill inside the old Salem Jail. Built in 1813, it was at one time the country's oldest active jail. Fast-forward to the present day and you'll find that this one hundred seat spot has stayed true to its roots. The dining room is decked out with a jail theme featuring brick walls, the original two foot thick granite floor and cell bars all around. Going well beyond bread and water, the menu is loaded with dishes that have prison related names, like the Al Capone featuring Italian sausage, broccoli rabe and fusilli or the Scarface with sauteed shrimp and linguini in a garlic parsley white wine sauce. The Mafia Steak is an entree Phantom can't refuse: fourteen ounces of perfectly grilled sirloin bathed in a cranberry port wine sauce.

Sabatino's

895 Main St., Wakefield, MA (781) 246-4444

Sabatino's is a family run Italian eatery offering old school recipes passed down from generation to generation. To keep the crowds coming back, the menu offers plenty of choice and superior value. An order of juicy double-cut pork chops with crispy potatoes and vinegar peppers costs under twenty bucks. The Italian platter for two overflows with enough veggies, meats and cheeses for four people. The signature Veal Grand Marnier features three tender slices dipped in egg batter, pan-fried and flambéed in an intoxicating orange sauce. Baked stuffed lasagna is stacked five inches high and blanketed in melted cheese. The loud but friendly environment usually overflows with locals in the know. Once the kitchen cools down, the bar heats up with multitudes of martinis.

Teresa's Italian Eatery

149 South Main St., Middleton, MA (978) 646-1111

www.teresaseatery.com

Teresa's is like the best pizza shop in town, the best sandwich shop in town and the best Italian restaurant in town all under one roof. The must try at Teresa's is the Pollo Milano. A golden fried Panko crusted chicken breast is topped with a tomato cream sauce that's so good, it will make you want to lick the plate. The Veal Papa is super tender, topped with buffalo mozzarella, prosciutto and roasted red peppers. The pizza at Teresa's is thin, crispy and delicious. There are classics like the Margherita with fresh mozzarella and basil or the Abbruzzi topped with red roasted peppers, ricotta and sausage. If you just want to swing by for cocktails, Teresa's has a separate martini lounge with a long list of creative drinks.

Toscana's Ristorante

3 Bourbon St., Peabody, MA (978) 535-0731

www.toscanaspeabody.com

Toscana's Ristorante is a family-run Italian eatery that's known for big portions of flavorful food. The restaurant is located at the end of a strip mall, but don't let the exterior fool you. Inside, you'll find a wide-open space with a newly expanded bar, white tablecloths and even live piano music. There's penne with sausage in a rich vodka cream sauce, hearty pasta Bolognese and perfectly executed fettuccini carbonara. The rack of lamb is grilled then baked to juicy perfection. The frutti di mare packs in an ocean full of seafood, topped with vibrant homemade marinara over a bed of linguini. Phantom's favorite dish is the Bistecca alla Toscana: a center cut sirloin stuffed with prosciutto, provolone and spinach topped with mushrooms and a sweet marsala wine sauce.

Portland
GREAT ATE

Duckfat

43 Middle St., Portland, ME (207) 774-8080

www.duckfat.com

Duckfat is a one of a kind Maine hangout that's part watering hole, part upscale sandwich shop and one hundred percent delicious. Located in a hip neighborhood, jazz plays overhead in the colorful dining room with exposed brick walls. The fun comfort food menu is lined with panini sandwiches, salads, milkshakes, homemade sodas and fried goodies. Local beers and wines round out the offerings. While everything on the menu is mouthwatering, a must have is their signature Belgian fries cooked in duck fat. They're insanely addictive, airy and earthy with decadent condiments like truffle ketchup and creamy horseradish mayo.

Fore Street

288 Fore St., Portland, ME (207) 775-2717

www.forestreet.biz

Whether it's grilled, roasted or simmered, every dish at Fore Street is an unparalleled success. Set in a former furniture factory with soaring ceilings, exposed brick walls and an amazing open kitchen, there's a definite energy and theatrical feel. It's rustic and casual, yet white lights make it a romantic setting. Copper tables line the soaring space, with a polished concrete bar dominating the lounge up front. From the huge wood-fired oven comes crispy, cracker-thin pizzas topped with goat cheese, while juicy rotisserie chickens do laps on the spit and the grill sizzles full of steaks, chops and fish. Phantom usually can't decide between the Wood Oven Roasted Mussels and the Spit Roasted Pork Loin.

Bayside Bowl

58 Alder St., Portland, ME (207) 791-2695

www.baysidebowl.com

Bayside Bowl is a twelve lane boutique bowling alley offering surprisingly sophisticated dining and an active bar. While the food at most lanes is mostly lame, the fare at Bayside is anything but with appetizers like BBQ Pork Cigars with braised pork deep fried inside crispy wontons or wings that are cooked on an open flame. Grilled pizzas and mac and cheese can be boosted with over twenty toppings. All the food can be ordered at Bayside's popular four-sided bar, in the dining room set with communal-style picnic tables or right at the lanes in the middle of all the action.

Becky's Diner

390 Commercial St., Portland, ME (207) 773-7070

www.beckysdiner.com

Located on Hobson's Wharf, Becky's Diner caters to hungry tables and packed counters with freshly caught seafood and classic diner plates. Breakfast is served for the bulk of the day. Pancakes are chock-full of local blueberries piled with plenty of Maine maple syrup. The Titanic omelette packs in enough food to sink a ship with four eggs, crispy bacon, ham, sausage, onions and peppers. Since Becky's has a lobster tank on-site, ordering Maine's favorite shellfish should be a no brainer, with twins coming in well below twenty-five bucks. Becky's is open 362 ½ days a year, taking time off only on Thanksgiving, Christmas and Christmas Eve.

Grace

15 Chestnut St., Portland, ME (207) 828-4422

www.restaurantgrace.com

Grace is a chic eatery built in a stunning 1850s Gothic Revival church. An open kitchen flanks the altar. The nave houses a thirty-five seat circular bar and diners are seated at austere wooden tables underneath the soaring cathedral ceiling hung with ornate chandeliers. The appealing menu focuses on seasonal and local ingredients, with upscale riffs on comfort food classics. Portions are moderate, yet richly flavored enough to satisfy. With most entrees around thirty dollars, god knows it's an inexpensive way to enjoy a special evening out.

Silly's

40 Washington Ave., Portland, ME (207) 772-0360

www.sillys.com

Silly's is as wacky as it's tasty, decorated with crazy lights, fun toys, interactive games and hundreds of photos of Silly's fans. "Silly" touches include menus kept in lunchboxes, water served in wine bottles and beer in old fashioned tin cups. The standout appetizers are the homemade sweet potato fries with honey mustard, hand cut "Danger Fries" with gravy, bacon and cheese, and the Rings of Fire featuring fried jalapenos with a cooling side of sour cream. Entrees are as tasty as they are whimsical, including the Greatest American Gyro and the Mary Had a Little Lamb Pizza topped with garlic, spinach, charbroiled lamb, feta, and capers. Silly's really shines when it comes to sweets, with over thirty different shakes in wild flavors like peanut butter and bacon.

David's Restaurant

22 Monument Sq., Portland, ME (207) 773-4340

www.davidsrestaurant.com

David's is a stylish eatery with exposed brick walls, original mosaic tiled floors and an in your face open kitchen. The energetic bar and dining room is filled with everyone from casual diners in jeans to couples decked out for a romantic night. Chef/owner David Turin has designed an approachable but certainly creative menu. There are inventive pizzas like the steak and lobster or the jerk chicken with goat cheese and arugula. The "Hands On" section of the menu has small plates of fried calamari, truffle fries and steak skewers that are great to share over cocktails. For a full meal, David's entree menu has everything from pepper crusted rare tuna to hearty meatloaf with crispy cumin onions. For the ultimate in value, Phantom loves feasting on "David's Lobster Dinner" which includes chowder, shrimp cocktail and Maine lobster with two sides for about thirty bucks.

The Grill Room & Bar

84 Exchange St., Portland, ME (207) 774-2333

www.hardingleesmith.com

Located in the Old Port district, the Grill Room & Bar is a restored space with century old brick walls decorated with antique meat cleavers. A long handcrafted bar runs along one wall with a great selection of beer, wine and cocktails. The five foot long grill fires steaks and seafood while the big, oak-fired oven is responsible for making their famous Wood Oven Roasted Half Chicken and pizzas like the Duck & Brie. Take advantage of both cooking methods when you order the tasty Maine mussels, roasted in the oven and served with bread right off the grill. Grilled meats and fish can be complimented by one of seventeen la carte sides, like Maine sea salt fries and truffle creamed spinach.

Providence
GREAT ATE

10 Prime Steak & Sushi

55 Pine St., Providence, RI (401) 453-2333

www.tenprimesteakandsushi.com

10 Prime Steak & Sushi is an underwater world of blue, wavelike structures with a cobalt backlit bar, Latin beats and erotic art that even made Phantom blush. Wildly patterned banquets, long shimmering curtains and dangling beaded lamps add to the sensual eye candy that consumes the narrow exposed brick space all the way back to the sushi bar. The menu features an unlikely combo of serious red meat and outrageously imaginative sushi, supplemented by fresh fish and amazing desserts. The steak house sides are truly special with dishes like the garlicky Death by Butter Potatoes loaded with Asiago, cream and a half a stick of butter melting on top. The 3D dessert menu comes with a pair of glasses so pictures of Crème Brulee and their 3 Chocolate Mousse seem to jump off the page.

Al Forno

577 South Main St., Providence, RI (401) 273-9760

www.alforno.com

Al Forno has a well-deserved international reputation, which helps explain why potential diners happily wait up to ninety minutes for a seat. White tablecloth dining takes place on two elegant levels with an ivory downstairs and a second floor decorated in slate stone tiles. Al Forno claims to be the inventor of the grilled pizza, featuring a wood-smoked, paper-thin crust topped with meticulously sourced imported olive oil, tomatoes, and cheeses. The kitchen also turns out oven baked dishes like rigatoni with five pepper sauce and roasted hot Italian sausages. All of this deliciousness is available Tuesday-Saturday for dinner only.

Costantino's Venda Ravioli

265 Atwells Ave., Providence, RI (401) 421-9105

www.vendaravioli.com

Costantino's Venda Ravioli is an Italian food emporium with everything you'd expect to find in a deli, cafe and specialty store. Their homemade pasta selection includes 250 fresh and frozen noodles. Ravioli are the specialty of the kitchen, stuffed with gourmet ingredients like lobster, spinach, basil, and ricotta. Phantom also flips for their tri-color cheese tortellini and the agnolotti with pine nuts, basil, and cheese. A huge four-sided deli case dominates the room, packed with cold cuts, butchered meats, an astounding assortment of olives and 100 cheeses. Venda serves lunch every afternoon at tables spread out around the store.

Bacaro

262 South Water St., Providence, RI (401) 751-3700

www.bacarorestaurant.com

Bacaro is a two floor restaurant with incredible views of downtown Providence, the waterfront, and their own open kitchen. They specialize in small bites called "cicchetti", Italian style tapas. There are bite sized panini filled with prosciutto and Taleggio cheese, fried olives stuffed with hearty Bolognese and pan seared scallops over truffled mushrooms. If you want to dine the more traditional way, Bacaro has entrees like Wood-Grilled Berkshire Pork Ribs or Pan-Fried Veal Tenderloin. For dessert, there are several flavors of ice cream churned in house and "Bella's Original Bombollini": little warm doughnuts filled with hazelnut-scented chocolate pastry cream dusted with powdered sugar.

Caserta Pizzeria

121 Spruce St., Providence, RI (401) 272-3618

www.casertapizzeria.com

What Pizzeria Regina is to the North End, Caserta Pizzeria is to Federal Hill, with old school charm, black and white tiled floors and seating you'd expect to see in a high school cafeteria. The menu is as simple as the surroundings, offering just pizza and calzones served on paper plates. Caserta is famous for the "Wimpy Skippy", which is essentially an open calzone stuffed with spinach, cheese and pepperoni. Other stuffed selections include the "Pig in a Blanket" with sweet Italian sausage or the "Pepper Pig", bursting with green bell pepper. Phantom is a huge Phan of the pizza, made with a sweet sauce and traditional toppings like hand cut pepperoni, mushrooms, olives and anchovies. Because they make their own dough, the crust is always crunchy. Dessert isn't offered, which is good because you probably won't have room for it anyway.

Mediterraneo

134 Atwells Ave., Providence, RI (401) 331-7760

www.mediterraneocaffe.com

Mediterraneo is a sleek, stylish Italian spot with al fresco seating that flows right into the dining room. Every dish on the menu is also spelled phonetically, so you'll have no problem when you want to order the caprese (CAH-PRAY-ZEH) or the Fusilli a la Vodka (FOO-ZEE-LEE AH-LA VAWD-CAH) . There are appetizers like the Antipasto Della Casa with the finest in cured meats, cheeses and grilled vegetables and the Gamberi Scampi sauteed in a garlic, parsley, lemon, and white wine butter sauce and served with grilled Tuscan bread. The cannelloni are stuffed with spinach and fresh ricotta and the Fruitti di Mare is packed with super fresh seafood. There are oversized lobster and ricotta filled ravioli finished in a light mascarpone pink sauce topped with extra large shrimp. For a little bit of both, there's a Surf and Turf with a tender filet served with two beautiful baked stuffed shrimp.

Duck & Bunny

312 Wickenden St., Providence, RI (401) 270-3300

www.theduckandbunny.com

The Duck & Bunny is a self-proclaimed 'snuggery', which basically is just a fancy word for a cozy, comfortable place. When you walk through the various rooms, you feel like Alice (the one from Wonderland) did the decorating. The place is clad in old-fashioned couches, ornate chandeliers and blazing fireplaces. Crepes are the house specialty, and they're anything but traditional. The kitchen makes everything from crepe pastas topped with Bolognese to crepe burritos and crepe sushi. There's even a crepe version of the classic New York System wiener, wrapped in a crepe and topped with meat sauce and yellow mustard. There are loads of creative cupcakes for dessert and a creative cocktail list.

Gracie's

194 Washington St., Providence, RI (401) 272-7811

www.graciesprovidence.com

Gracie's is an intimate eatery with rich woodwork, high ceilings and candles to create a very warm, comfortable experience. You can grab a drink in the lounge before heading to dine on a wonderfully diverse American menu. There's an a la carte prix fixe option where you can choose between starters like handmade russet potato gnocchi or mussels with smoked chorizo. Main dishes range from rigatoni with sausage to ocean fresh Atlantic halibut. Carnivores will be impressed by the all-natural Black Angus ribeye served with triple cooked potatoes and Swiss chard (grown in their rooftop garden). Round out the three course experience with one of Gracie's artful desserts such as the Madagascar vanilla bean crème brulee.

South End
GREAT ATE

Stella

1525 Washington St., Boston, MA (617) 247-7747

www.bostonstella.com

This posh restaurant and buzzing bar are easy on the eyes with a polished, all-white interior that's highly designed and quite modern. Italian fine dining is executed perfectly with grilled pizzas, homemade pasta and a late night menu served until 1:30am. Simple dishes like the spaghetti tossed with toasted garlic, olive oil and Parmesan are always fresh and flavorful. Portions aren't overly ample and seem tailor-made for the slim, stylish waistlines around the room. Stella has a small cafe adjacent to the restaurant that serves breakfast and lunch until mid-afternoon.

Union Bar and Grille

1357 Washington St., Boston, MA (617) 423-0555

www.unionrestaurant.com

Union Bar and Grille turns out urban comfort food for the stylish soul. The gothic-meets-urban scene combines massive wrought iron chandeliers and black leather banquettes, and the small bar area is framed in floor-to-ceiling glass and slanted mirrors. The menu is on the forefront of creativity with dishes like lobster cavatelli with heirloom zucchini and tiny tomatoes. The 24 Hour Brisket Sandwich is served with horseradish on a pretzel roll. Almost every one of their delicious desserts is capped with homemade ice cream in wild flavors like Marcona almond, ginger or blood orange.

Estragon

700 Harrison Ave., Boston, MA (617) 266-0443

www.estragontapas.com

Estragon is a swanky Spanish tapas joint clad with plush couches, red lighting and daring drinkers sipping cava sparkling wine straight from the bottle. The owner is from Madrid and serves the food he grew up with like the Flamenquines: tender pork that's pounded out, stuffed with Serrano and Manchego, breaded and deep fried. For the less adventurous, the hamburgesa is made with Kobe beef and Spanish cheeses. Estragon is only open for dinner, but its neighboring sister sandwich shop, Las Ventas, makes amazingly authentic bocadillos packed with tasty meats and fresh vegetables for lunch.

Coda Bar & Kitchen

329 Columbus Ave., Boston MA (617) 536-2632

www.codaboston.com

Coda serves dolled-up comfort food in an urban setting at suburban prices. The menu is concise but well thought out, with approachable offerings galore. Portions are generous but not so over-the-top that you'll be tempted to skip dessert. Appetizers like grilled beef skewers with tzatziki or spicy calamari are always under ten dollars and entrees like mac and cheese with pancetta and peas or the smoked bone-in pork chop are well below twenty. Coda is easy to find, just a few steps from Back Bay Station on the corner of COlumbus and DArtmouth (hence the name). But, good luck finding visitor's parking in this neighborhood.

Kitchen

560 Tremont St., Boston, MA (617) 695-1250

www.kitchenbostonmass.com

Kitchen is a cozy subterranean nook with al fresco dining for the spring and summer. The menu reads like a history book, with recipes that date mostly from the late nineteenth century. However, there's nothing tired or dated about this place. There's the original hamburger, the Hamburg Steak, served with crunchy onion shoestrings. The Lobster Thermidor is ultra-rich and filling, packed with chunks of meat and gnocchi in a creamy, cheesy sauce. The dessert menu is lined with yummy throwbacks like crème brulee, toffee pudding and doughnuts. For a more intimate experience, ask for a table in the back overlooking the outdoor garden.

Orinoco

477 Shawmut Ave., Boston, MA (617) 369-7075

22 Harvard St., Brookline, MA (617) 232-9505

56 JFK St., Cambridge, MA (617) 354-6900

www.orinocokitchen.com

Orinoco is a casual, charming Venezuelan restaurant decorated with a carnival of color. The menu includes family recipes served with South American wines, beers and specialty drinks. This is the ultimate spot for dining on arepas, Venezuelan sandwiches served on grilled corn bread that's stuffed with moist chunks of chicken, flavorful shredded beef or tender slices of pork. There are larger entrees under twenty dollars like the plantain crusted mahi mahi. For dessert, the only dish you need to know is the molten chocolate cake. Brunch is served on Sundays with both American and Venezuelan-style breakfast items.

El Centro

472 Shawmut St., Boston, MA (617) 262-5708

El Centro is a cool Mexican eatery with a dimly lit dining room donned in colorful knickknacks and cool art on exposed brick walls. There are only five bar seats, so this is a more relaxed, authentic Mexican experience than Tex-Mex restaurants full of patrons pounding margaritas. To start, the guacamole is a must try, especially with chorizo and cheese. There's a variety of tacos stuffed with fillings like charcoal grilled steak or pork loin with pineapple. Phantom recommends the addictive shrimp wrapped in bacon and stuffed with cheese, as well as a do it yourself carne asada served with fresh corn tortillas made on-site. The ultimate way to end your meal at El Centro is the churros and chocolate.

Mike's City Diner

1714 Washington St., Boston, MA (617) 267-9393

www.mikescitydiner.com

At Mike's City Diner, there are black and white checkered tabletops, counter stools overlooking a hot griddle and oldies playing overhead. This fun neighborhood mainstay has been serving homestyle diner classics for seventeen years. Phantom loves their blueberry pancakes, layered in fat, fluffy, bronze-topped short stacks with sweet-tart patches of fruit. The American breakfast menu sizzles with eggs, waffles, pork sausages, and real Southern grits (which is a rarity for a Boston restaurant). The homemade hash mixes potato cubes with beefy corned beef under two fried eggs. There are tons of specialty sandwiches, triple-decker clubs and beefy burgers to feast on at lunch. Note: Mike's is only open until 3pm.

South of Boston
GREAT ATE

Alma Nove

22 Shipyard Dr., Hingham, MA (781) 749-3353

www.almanovehingham.com

Located in the Hingham Shipyard, Alma Nove sports a bright and airy dining room and a gorgeous outdoor patio featuring a warm and inviting fire pit. Chef Paul Wahlberg (yes, those Wahlbergs) has created an Italian/Mediterranean menu with entrees like the rigatoni with Italian sausage, roasted eggplant and fresh mozzarella, tomato and basil or the all natural sirloin steak with a red wine demi-glace. There's wood-grilled swordfish served with lobster mashed potatoes and appetizers like braised pork meatballs with smoked paprika and coriander over creamy polenta. The desserts are delicious, like the honey vanilla creme brulee and chocolate sour cream cake topped with chocolate ganache, served in a pool of vanilla anglaise.

Tosca

14 North St., Hingham, MA (781) 740-0080

www.toscahingham.com

Tosca has a dark, dramatic setting created by rough exposed brick, mahogany beams and lofty ceilings. Stained glass lamps in shades of glowing amber, extravagant tiles and an open kitchen give the room upscale distinction. The wood oven adds a rustic complexity to many of the pastas, meats and pizzas. The menu is devotedly Italian with pasta and pizza, but there's also good use of New England seafood. Portions are on the heavy side, with equal parts quantity and full-bodied flavor. Tosca is housed in the 1910 Granary Marketplace building in Hingham's North Square, so there's plenty of parking.

Oysters Bar & Grill

254 Church St., Pembroke, MA (781) 924-1065

www.oystersbarandgrille.com

Oysters Bar & Grill is in a strip mall and doesn't look like much from the outside. However, inside you'll find a bright, cheery dining room with a slightly nautical theme and a chef/owner who's always in the kitchen. There's an inviting bar where you can watch bartenders shaking cocktails and shucking oysters. Most everything on the menu is made on-site, including all the breads, pastas and ice creams. Some of the standout dishes include seafood fra diavolo packed with mussels, shrimp and scallops over handmade pasta or swordfish picatta with lemon and capers. There are locally inspired dishes like New England Bouillabaisse or Portuguese clams with white wine and linguica. The juicy steak frites feature hand cut Parmesan fries and the enormous all natural beef burger is topped with Vermont cheddar cheese on a homemade brioche bun. Things get even more delicious at dessert with an ultra-rich chocolate chip bread pudding and hot donuts served with homemade espresso ice cream.

Sintra

906 Washington St., Braintree, MA (781) 848-1151

www.sintrarestaurant.com

Sintra is a posh, romantic spot that's been serving Mediterranean comfort food for nearly a decade. This eatery may be named for a city in Portugal, but this is NOT a Portuguese restaurant with dishes like the mustard glazed pork chop or the tender New York sirloin with whipped potatoes. A great starter to share is the hot sampler featuring baked oysters, clams casino, a cod cake and an enormous crab cake. Sintra also has plenty of pasta dishes like baked rigatoni with chorizo or the creative "broken ravioli", featuring shrimp scampi and a big, thin sheet of house made pasta on top. While this is certainly a place for a beautiful sit down dinner, there's also a happening bar for a beer and some gourmet Buffalo chicken dip.

Tavern at Quarry Hills

100 Quarry Ln., Quincy, MA (617) 689-1900

www.granitelinksgolfclub.com

This casual American bistro at the Granite Links Golf Club overlooks 450 acres of rolling fairways, trees and ponds with the most spectacular view of the Boston skyline you've ever seen. The Tavern serves the kind of menu Phantom Phans love, like crispy steak and cheese spring rolls with shredded prime rib, and Black Angus burgers with fries. The huge club sandwiches are prepared with fresh roasted turkey and honey maple bacon. For something to share, there are incredible grilled pizzas topped with everything from chicken and pesto to sausage, peppers and onions. Whether you're outside on the patio or inside the dining room or lounge, it's hard to concentrate on the view when the food is this good.

Orta

75 Washington St., Pembroke, MA (781) 826-8883

www.ortarestaurant.com

Named for a lake in the Piedmont region of Italy, Orta has a warm and inviting dining room. The open kitchen brings energy and excitement to the space with a wood burning brick pizza oven. Customers get a chance to watch the amazing entrees like braised beef short ribs or lobster stuffed sole come off the line. If there's one appetizer you have to order, it's definitely the mini arancini served with a spicy tomato sauce. If you want to get really close to the action, grab a seat at Orta's pizza bar where you can witness the chef create authentic Neapolitan style pies like the Margherita, with buffalo mozzarella, basil and a drizzle of olive oil.

Rose Alley

94 Front St., New Bedford, MA (508) 858-5123

www.drinkrosealley.com

From the outside, you wouldn't expect this historic building would have a bar with forty craft beers on draft and a lineup of rock solid food to go with it. There are Buffalo chicken egg rolls, homemade potato chips smothered with chili, cheese, bacon and jalapenos and boneless wings that can be coated in eight dry rubs and tossed with over a dozen sauces. The craziest dish on the menu is called Vavo's Hangover Cure. It's packed with shrimp and chicken in a spicy saffron sauce served atop a mound of pub style potato chips that promises to soak up everything that ails you. All this food can be enjoyed at one of the high top tables or at the bar in the center of the dining room.

42 Degrees North

690 State Rd., Manomet MA (508) 224-1500

www.42degreesnorthrestaurant.com

Off the beaten path, in the Manomet section of Plymouth, 42 Degrees North is a cool, nautical style restaurant with a casual bar to enjoy cocktails and an outdoor patio for the nice weather. The menu is lined with large portions at reasonable prices. The crab cakes are a great start, full of real Chesapeake lump crabmeat. Spicy little neck clams are sauteed with chorizo, roasted corn and scallions and the 42 Degrees House Meatballs are an unexpected Italian treat. Other popular dishes include bacon wrapped shrimp with bucatini pasta, a chargrilled ribeye topped with smoked bacon butter and a short rib stuffed hamburger. Since they're in Plymouth, fresh seafood is a must and the selection changes daily based on what their local fish monger catches. Diners can choose to have their fish fried, blackened, grilled, pan-seared or broiled.

Theater District
GREAT ATE

Davio's

75 Arlington St., Boston, MA (617) 357-4810

236 Patriot Pl., Foxboro, MA (508) 339-4810

www.davios.com

Davio's is Phantom's favorite Italian steak house. The huge open kitchen puts out chops and aged Prime beef along with antipasti and red sauce pasta. Creative starters include four types of spring rolls like the Philly cheese steak, chicken parm, Buffalo chicken and shrimp cotija. For entrees, the grilled porterhouse veal chop is an impressive cut of meat. Phantom's hands down favorite is the prime Kobe Beef rib eye with a few a la carte sides like creamy mashed potatoes, freshly shucked corn or portobello mushrooms in aged balsamic. There's an in-house bakery whipping up desserts, pastries, and oven-fresh breads. Thick interior columns and wide windows mark the spacious, elegant setting, and the open wine room displays 300 selections.

Pigalle

75 Charles St., South Boston, MA (617) 423-4944

www.pigalleboston.com

Pigalle is a handsome black and tan setting with slim columns and ceiling arches that draw the eye toward vintage chandeliers and beaded sconces. Curved leather banquettes and a six seat bar add to the delightfully intimate space. James Beard award winning chef Marc Orfaly gives locals and tourists the taste of fine French, Mediterranean and Asian influenced cuisine. For an affordable sample of this world class fare, check out their forty dollar, multi-coursed pre-theatre prix fixe menu. Parking is validated at the Revere Hotel parking lot.

Fleming's

217 Stuart St., Boston, MA (617) 292-0808

One West Exchange St., Providence, RI (401) 533-9000

www.flemingssteakhouse.com

Fleming's Prime Steakhouse upgrades the standard chain experience with professional service and masculine atmosphere. Rich cherry wood, wine bottles, and red leather booths fill the dimly lit room between the spacious bar and an open kitchen. The a la carte menu has a solid selection of prime corn-fed beef, plus fresh seafood and a remarkable 100 wines by the glass. Steak portions range in size from eight to forty ounces, offering as much flexibility as the wine list. Start with the Chilled Seafood Tower piled with lobster, shrimp and crab for a truly opulent experience. If you're at the Boston location, skip the valet and save some cash by parking at the Motor Mart Garage at 26 Park Plaza, which is validated.

Teatro

177 Tremont St., Boston, MA (617) 778-6841

www.teatroboston.com

Teatro, which means "theater" in Italian, is a stunning space. The arched, ornate barrel ceiling is gorgeous, cast with soft blue lighting that hangs like heavy applause. The restaurant is a fabulous choice for fine Northern Italian dining with options like thin crust pizza topped with hot peppers and sea salt. The rigatoni with ragu Bolognese is classic and meaty, and the grilled ribeye comes with Gorgonzola butter. Most of the high decibel buzz comes from the bar, where one-of-a-kind cocktails include the limoncello laced Carlini Tini.

Troquet

140 Boylston St., Boston, MA (617) 695-9463

www.troquetboston.com

Overlooking Boston Common, Troquet is a smart setting of burgundy walls lined with mirrors to give the sleek, intimate room a more spacious feel. Phantom gives a standing ovation to their rotating selection of fine wines by the glass. Four dozen choices are listed down the center of the menu, with matching dishes off to the sides. Wines can be sampled in two and four ounce pours. As for bottles, there are 350 varieties. The open kitchen prepares fabulous wine-friendly French and Italian cuisine like foie gras and roasted venison.

Vapiano

191 Stuart St., Boston, MA (857) 445-0236

www.vapianointernational.com

Located in the heart of the Theater District, Vapiano is all about food that's fast, fresh, affordable and delicious. The concept at Vapiano is a little different. Customers get a chip card that keeps a running tab of whatever they order from the pasta, panini and pizza stations. The atmosphere is cool and comfortable with communal tables, hardwood floors, and even a tree right in the dining room. It's the kind of place where you can grab a quick bite or linger all day long over a beer straight from the tap or with an indulgent personal sized portion of tiramisu.

Market by Jean-George

100 Stuart St., Boston, MA (617) 310-6790

www.marketbyjgboston.com

Market is a chic, bustling eatery and the brainchild of superstar chef Jean-Georges Vongerichten. The centerpiece of the W Hotel's soaring atrium lobby, the sleek, modular design of glass and steel offers spectacular city views from every seat in the dining room. The tightly edited menu features prime local ingredients dolled up with French techniques and Asian flavors. Portions are huge compared to most haute cuisine with ample dishes like the Parmesan-Crusted Chicken or the Ginger-Scented Lobster. Elegant endings include a terrific crème fraîche cheesecake doused with cherry compote and sour-cherry sorbet.

Montein

63 Stuart St., Boston, MA (617) 338-5600

www.montien-boston.com

Montien is more elegant and accessible than the Chinatown competition nearby. Pale peach walls, giant open windows and a curvaceous, dark wood bar frame the tiny space, with pretty plants around the room and cozy seats tucked into alcoves along one wall. Two Thai menus are available: one that's uber-authentic and another more Americanized version. So, if you want the less watered down menu, ask for your food "Thai style". There's a sushi bar that's small in size but huge in offerings. The staff is great about getting theater customers in and out before their show starts.

Strega Waterfront

56 Northern Ave., Boston, MA (617) 345-3992

www.stregawaterfront.com

North End restaurateur Nick Varano has upgraded his Italian dining concept at Fan Pier on the Boston waterfront. The design of the dining room is unlike anything Boston has ever seen with elegant chandeliers, an intimate fireplace and killer views of Boston Harbor. There's a high tech lounge full of flat screens with a Vegas-style atmosphere. The lobster fra diavolo is a must order, made with fresh pasta in a spicy tomato sauce. Other Italian favorites include the deep sea scallops sauteed with sweet Grand Marnier, a towering salad stacked with layers of crispy fried eggplant, fresh mozzarella cheese, and vine-ripe tomatoes, and Strega's legendary twenty ounce veal chop.

606 Congress

606 Congress St., Boston, MA (617) 476-5606

www.606congress.com

Inside the sparking Renaissance Boston Waterfront Hotel, 606 Congress is a soaring space featuring a sleek design, floor to ceiling wine towers and a state of the art open kitchen. The cuisine ranges from fancy to fun, with dishes like Lobster Eggs Benedict for breakfast or the Chicken Pretzel Panini with bacon and Swiss for lunch. At dinner, Phantom goes for the butter poached lobster with goat cheese stuffed ravioli. The most decadent dessert is the hot chocolate pudding with orange ginger and dried chilis.

Rosa Mexicano

155 Seaport Blvd., Boston, MA (617) 476-6122

www.rosamexicano.com

Over the past twenty-five years, Rosa Mexicano has built an empire of upscale Mexican eateries stretching from New York City to South Beach. They've now set up a Boston location with a colorful ambiance, an unquenchable bar scene and eye-catching water walls with cliff-diving figurines that leap right out at you. This 300 seat restaurant has seating both indoors and out. Phantom starts by ordering a big bowl of guacamole prepared tableside. From there, you can dig into a sampler of fresh made tuna and scallop ceviche or try a flight of gourmet tacos. Larger entrees include eighteen ounces of grilled short ribs in a tomato chipotle sauce or the marinated Niman Ranch skirt steak served with shrimp and hand cut Mexican style garlic fries.

Pasta Beach Italian Restaurant & Bar

30 Rowes Wharf, Boston, MA (617) 439-6900

7 Memorial Blvd., Newport, RI (401) 847-2222

www.pastabeachrestaurants.com

Pasta Beach is an inviting, open eatery with high ceilings and huge windows overlooking a patio of additional seating. The elegant dining room is dimly lit with a counter that looks right into a semi open kitchen. Everything has been brought in from Italy, including their chef who whips real Neapolitan pizza in an 850 degree oven. The Bolognese is thick and meaty, served over fresh pasta. The Veal Milanese takes up most of the plate, pounded thin and served with a wedge of lemon to squeeze on top. House made meringues are crunchy and sweet, topped with fresh strawberries and whipped cream. Pasta Beach is a triple threat, serving breakfast, lunch and dinner seven days a week. There's a second location in Newport, RI.

Temazcal Tequila Cantina

250 Northern Ave., Boston, MA (617) 439-3502

www.temazcalcantina.com

Just feet away from the harbor, Temazcal is Spanish for "House of Heat", and the bar scene definitely sizzles. The always active dining room has huge windows right on the Atlantic and is usually packed with post work pretty people slinging back stiff cocktails. The iPad menus list dish after dish of authentic Mexican fare, an extensive wine list and three hundred tequilas. Scanning through the offerings, you'll find bacon-wrapped shrimp with chorizo, prime beef tenderloin in a blanket of melted cheese, grilled chicken with a topical salsa and tortilla soup served with a smorgasbord of toppings.

Trade

540 Atlantic Ave., Boston MA (617) 451-1234

www.trade-boston.com

Located on Boston's Greenway, not far from the water, Trade serves small plates and creative cocktails just outside the Financial District. The action never stops at the busy kitchen bar where flatbreads are cooked crispy and rigatoni is baked bubbly in a wood stone oven. Fun appetizers that can be enjoyed at the bar over post work cocktails include fried dough topped with prosciutto, Parmesan and anchovies or the pork lettuce wraps with a chili dipping sauce. Phantom loves to feast on upscale dishes like the grilled Pineland Farm skirt with a house steak sauce. Trade's dining room is dimly lit, while the bar is lively and loud.

Empire

1 Marina Park Dr., Boston, MA (617) 295-0001

(55 Northern Ave. for GPS)

www.empireboston.com

From the folks who brought us Red Lantern comes the latest and greatest in over the top Asian. This enormous establishment is decked out to the nines with blue and red velvet couches, scantily clad servers, Chinese lanterns and a huge open kitchen where sushi is sliced and woks toss noodles and rice. The menu offers creative spins on sushi like the Lobster Salad Roll or the Fish and Chips Roll. There are loads of things for meat lovers like steak frites and Korean rubbed sirloin. Noodles, pho and clay pot dishes are offered for a more Pan Asian meal. After you're done dining, you'll want to make your way to the bar area which is always a scene. This is a swanky establishment, so it has a dress code. Phantom suggests leaving your flip flops and tank tops at home.

No Name

15 Fish Pier St. West, South Boston, MA (617) 338-7539

www.nonamerestaurant.com

Everything about this casual family style restaurant is as simple and straightforward as its humble name. The 200 seat dining room has wood walls and a nautical theme. Tables are set with placemats depicting how to eat a lobster. The dining room overlooks the harbor, and in the distance you can watch planes taking off from Logan. Some of those planes might be delivering seafood to restaurants around the country. Since No Name is located right on the Pier, the fish have a much shorter commute so you know it's fresh. The semi-open kitchen cranks out some of the best broiled, fried and sauteed seafood in the city. The lunch and dinner menus are the same, with prices way below the neighboring restaurants. No matter what time you dine at No Name, the huge portions and free parking make the meal amazingly affordable.

Worcester
GREAT ATE

The Boynton

117 Highland St., Worcester, MA (508) 756-5432

www.boyntonrestaurant.com

The Boynton is a loud, lively haunt catering to college students and young families. The cozy dining room is awash in warm colors, low lighting and exposed brick. The menu is a hodgepodge of burgers, pizza, fried seafood, barbecue, meatloaf, Italian and just about everything else. To start, there are waffle-cut Cajun fries dripping with melted cheese, salsa and sour cream. The seafood platter boasts a veritable mountain of crispy fried haddock, shrimp, scallops and clams, served with potato wedges and house made coleslaw. The best dish on the menu comes at the end. The Boynton Brown Betty is a piping hot piece of fried dough covered with apples, caramel and ice cream. Nothing costs more than twenty-two bucks (and that's for the filet!).

Brew City Grill & Brew House

104 Shrewsbury St., Worcester, MA (508) 752-3862

www.brew-city.com

Brew City is somewhat of a misnomer because it doesn't brew its own beer, but it does have forty varieties on tap. It's more of a sports bar featuring several TVs scattered amongst steel pipework and lighting. If you want a creative burger, this is your place. The Crunch Burger is made with potato chips and aged provolone. The King Burger is topped with bacon, grilled banana and peanut butter. If you like to experiment with your own flavor combinations, Brew City offers five types of buns, five different burgers and thirty-nine toppings. Beyond burgers, there's a big menu of sandwiches, salads and entrees infused with beer like the Guinness battered fish and chips or the stout braised short ribs.

Ceres Bistro

363 Plantation St., Worcester, MA (508) 754-2000

www.ceresbistro.com

Ceres Bistro at the Beechwood Hotel is maybe the coolest, classiest, most creative restaurant in Central Massachusetts. There's a stained glass dome on the ceiling, high-tech lighting that electrifies the bar, a beautiful patio and a kitchen firing sophisticated fare. Breakfast, lunch and dinner are served on a menu that changes with the seasons. Fresh oysters come with a champagne mignonette. Appetizers like the "Bacon & Eggs", which includes crispy pork belly, cheddar grits and a fried egg, are playful but upscale. There are also signature dishes like the ultimate bistro classic: Steak Frites.

One Eleven Chop House

111 Shrewsbury St., Worcester, MA (508) 799-4111

www.111chophouse.com

One Eleven Chop House is a flurry of activity from the flashy open kitchen to the horseshoe bar. The vast, tiered room looks more brasserie than steak house, with vintage French posters and suspended stained glass lighting. This chop house is full of non-traditional surprises like sushi and some Asian appetizers. Phantom always starts out with some fresh oysters and cherrystones. From there, One Eleven offers a traditional wedge salad with crumbled Stilton cheese. Pretty much every cut of steak is on the menu like filet mignon wrapped in applewood smoked bacon or the dry aged New York sirloin. Plus, there are more than ten sides to order a la carte.

Wonder Bar

121 Shrewsbury St., Worcester, MA (508) 752-9909

www.wonderbarrestaurant.net

The family run Wonder Bar has been a Worcester institution for decades. Mustard colored tables, brown booths and wood paneling have a dated look that locals and old timers wouldn't trade for anything. Decorations like a pizza shaped guitar and rock star photos give the place character. Their salute to Italian pizza starts with a medium thick crust slathered in tangy sauce and cheese with traditional toppings. Pizzas come in one bar pie size: an individual six slice round that Phantom finishes in one sitting. Beware, Wonder Bar is closed on Mondays.

El Basha

258 Park Ave., Worcester, MA (508) 795-0222

424 Belmont St., Worcester, MA (508) 797-0884

2 Connector Rd., Westboro, MA (508) 366-2455

www.elbasharestaurant.com

El Basha has a charming dining room with ceilings painted like blue skies and murals on the walls depicting scenes of Middle Eastern ruins. An opulent gold and crystal chandelier hangs from the ceiling, while palm trees huddle in the corner. The Lebanese menu stays true to its culture with grains, grilled meats and bean purees. Scrumptious Kibbee Balls are made with spiced ground beef and bulger wheat compacted and browned in olive oil until crispy. The kabobs feature moist morsels of grilled chicken, steak or lamb on a bed of rice pilaf. Delicious falafel is drizzled with a wonderfully creamy tahini sauce. For dessert, the sweet and tasty baklava is layer upon layer of honey soaked chopped pecans with paper-thin phyllo. There's a small parking lot adjacent to the Belmont Street location.

Gumbo

65 Water St., Worcester, MA (508) 926-8353

www.gumboworcester.com

Gumbo is a taste of New Orleans right in Central Mass. The space is divided into three rooms: a fun bar to catch jazz or blues, a smaller oyster bar where the bivalves are shucked right in front of you, and an intimate dining room where a fireplace blazes and light peeks through an ornate glass window. The kitchen is serious about Cajun and Creole food, cranking out jambalaya, etouffee, blackened meats and fish and of course, gumbo. Other foods from The Big Easy include shrimp and eggplant beignets, filling po'boys and fried green tomatoes.

EVO Dining

234 Chandler St., Worcester, MA (508) 459-4240

www.evodining.com

EVO Dining is a swanky, sleek eatery with big leather booths and stone columns. The menu is full of comfort foods from around the globe. You'll find Italian, Mexican, Indian, Lebanese, Asian and even good old American BBQ. The perfect starter to share is the EVO Sampler with crunchy eggrolls, creamy spinach and artichoke dip, classic chicken fingers, tangy bruschetta dip and arancini. Burgers are big, especially the "PHAT Albert" which has two plump patties stuffed with a blend of cheeses and wrapped in foil to keep it from falling apart. Breakfast with that same global mindset is available on the weekends, offering dishes like Italian French toast and breakfast burritos.

AAA Southern New England is proud of our partnership with The Phantom Gourmet team. Phantom Gourmet is New England's #1 source of food and fun on television and radio providing advice and tips on the dining choices in the communities in which we live and work.

Now that you have the Phantom's Guide to Boston's Best Restaurants, think about picking up a few Phantom Gourmet Restaurant Gift cards available at all AAA Southern New England branches where Members receive a 10% Discount!

Your AAA membership also serves as your special passport to other valuable benefits, services and discounts.

Did you know AAA is also a full service Travel Agency? When you plan and book with AAA Travel, you are eligible for exclusive Member Benefits.

Whether you are looking for cruise, land tour, honeymoon, family vacation or a quick getaway with friends, we have vacations to fit your style and budget. Our experienced Travel Counselors will find the best accommodations, most creative itineraries, and anything else you need to make your vacation memorable.

Go on, you deserve it! Call AAA Travel today and get excited about your next great vacation!

1-800-222-7448 • **AAA.com** • **AAA Branches**

Our AAA team averages 5,480 assists every day!

AAA delivers the best roadside assistance available anywhere, 24/7/365. Not only that, but we help members score huge savings on everything from retail stores to travel and lodging; from movie tickets to insurance; from financial services to theme parks and attractions. With so many **discounts and world class services**, Membership can pay for itself many times over! And that's a big help.

We are committed to helping and serving our neighbors and communities.

If you're not already a member, what are you waiting for?

1-800-JOIN-AAA • AAA.com/join

Index of Restaurants by Location

Alphabetical Index

Supplied by Community Energy